The Art of Tuba and Euphonium

by Harvey Phillips and William Winkle

ISBN-10: 0-87487-682-6
ISBN-13: 978-0-87487-682-6

King Model 2341 Tuba photo provided by United Musical Instruments U.S.A., Inc.
Yamaha YEP 321 Euphonium Photo provided by Yamaha Corporation of America

CONTENTS

PREFACE

This book serves the need for an authoritative guide to the euphonium and tuba for students, teachers, and professional performers. The content and presentation of the book as applied to the wind instruments is clearly stated. Detailed discussion includes considerations for all levels of performance. Appendices include study materials recommended for beginner, intermediate, and advanced levels. They also present a pictorial history of the evolution and development of the tuba/euphonium family and a selected list of outstanding artists who represent our heritage.

This is a valuable addition to existing books on brass instruments and is an indispensable guide to artistic, technical, and practical aspects of the tuba and euphonium for both teachers and players.

Dr. Arnold M. Jacobs
Retired Tubist
Chicago Symphony Orchestra

ACKNOWLEDGMENTS

We herewith acknowledge our many friends and colleagues who encouraged the writing of this book. Their steady support and enthusiasm were inspirational.

Most especially we thank our respective families for their patience and understanding through the hours of research, discussions, and proofreading.

Chapter 1

HISTORY OF THE TUBA AND RELATED INSTRUMENTS

According to eminent musicologist Curt Sachs, all wind instruments are correctly classified as aerophones. Simply stated, an aerophone is a tube or pipe (either open or closed) enclosing a column of air and acting as a sound resonator. All brass instruments, including the tuba family, are lip-vibrated aerophones. This term thus identifies those musical instruments that produce sound when players project air through their lips, causing them to vibrate into a cup-shaped mouthpiece that channels the vibrating air stream into the pipe or tube. In combination, the length of tube, tension of the lips, and speed and direction of the air stream determine the pitch produced.

It is interesting to note that instruments of the brass family are not classified together because they are fabricated from a common metal or alloy but because they all produce sounds by vibrating lips into a cup-shaped mouthpiece. This factor establishes brass instruments as the most "physical" of wind instruments.

All brass instruments are designated as having a cylindrical or a conical bore. Cylindrical instruments maintain consistent bore size throughout the major portion of their length with a slight taper in the leadpipe section and a major taper in the bell section as it flares to form the bell. Cylindrical instruments have a characteristic brilliant tone quality (this group includes trumpets and trombones). Conical bore instruments have a gradual taper for the major portion of their length, including the leadpipe and bell sections, and have cylindrical tubing through the valve section (including attached tubing and crooks for ease in tuning each valve). Some conical instruments, both historic and modern, maintain a degree of conical taper through the valve section and appropriate crooks. Conical instruments produce a characteristic mellow tone quality (this group includes the cornet, fluegelhorn, horn, euphonium, and all other members of the tuba family).

The earliest predecessors of modern brass instruments were conch shells, rams horns, hollow wooden pipes, and other objects provided by nature. These primitive instruments became important for communicating signals of special meaning over distances beyond the range of the human voice and for accompanying various tribal ceremonies. In Greek mythology, the "conch horn" was blown by the Tritons; the rams horn, or "shofar," is traditionally used in Jewish rituals, sounded on solemn occasions, and to this day is used in the observance of Rosh Hoshana and Yom Kippur; Aborigines of New Guinea and Australia still use an instrument made from a hollow limb, the "dijeridu," to accompany funeral and mourning ceremonies as well as for joyous occasions.

Early brass instruments and their predecessors were essentially "bugles," limited to producing tonal pitches of the overtone series. (Chapter 5 elaborates on specifics of the overtone series as related to the tuba family). The absence of valves on early brass instruments influenced players and composers to exploit overtones in the upper ranges of these instruments, thus utilizing the greater flexibility and choice of possible tones. As is the case with modern players, the capacity of an individual to produce music on a particular instrument depended on the extent of his ability to develop skill and control and to fully explore the potential of that instrument.

The serpent is perhaps the earliest known bass wind instrument considered to be a direct predecessor to the tuba and euphonium. Early serpents were simple conical tubes of wood covered with leather and coiled in such fashion that the tone holes could be reached conveniently. Keys were added later to facilitate improved performance technique. The serpent used a shallow cup-shaped mouthpiece usually made of ivory and about the size of a modern euphonium mouthpiece. Primarily used to reinforce the bass voices of vocal choirs, the serpent is a fairly soft-spoken instrument, lacking the dynamic range to become a full-fledged member of the symphony orchestra. Consequently, composers wrote very little for the instrument in that medium. Efforts to improve the serpent led naturally to the development of the ophicléide. Made of brass, the ophicléide resembled a large metal bassoon with tone holes in the side covered by padded keys. It was played with a cup- or funnel-shaped mouthpiece, usually made of metal or ivory. More powerful than the serpent, the ophicleide soon gained prominent and challenging roles in many orchestral compositions, especially in works by Mendelssohn, Berlioz, and Wagner. The ophicléide is the most important and most immediate in the lineage of instruments that prompted the development of the tuba. Most notably, however, it was the invention and utilization of the valve on brass instruments that brought about fabrication of the first tuba.

Modern brass instruments are made chromatic by the seven possible combinations of a basic set of three valves. Each of these seven positions is, in effect, a bugle on which the player (to the limit of his physical ability) can produce the pitches of an ascending overtone series. The crossovers and/or duplications of overtones made possible by the seven valve combinations provide choices of intonation and the instrument's response. The lack of valves on early brass instruments severely limited the chromatic potential of those instruments. The desire of both players and composers for more chromaticism in the middle and lower ranges led to the orderly innovations of tone holes (cornetto, shawn, serpent, etc.) and eventual development and refinement of piston and rotary valves.

Available information regarding the development or invention of a workable valve indicates that in 1815 a Prussian horn player named Heinrich Stölzel became the first to apply such a device to a brass instrument. Stölzel demonstrated a horn equipped with two square valves, one of which lowered the pitch one half step and the other of which lowered the pitch one whole step.

He played a solo on such a two-valve horn in a concert at Leipzig in December 1817.[1] The actual inventor of the valve as we know it today will most likely never be known for certain, owing to a controversy surrounding the invention. Although Heinrich Stölzel and Friedrich Blühmel jointly patented a spring-operated square piston valve in 1818 in Berlin, they each later claimed to be the sole inventor. Soon after the Stölzel-Blühmel valve horn went into production in Berlin (ca. 1818), Shuster of Carlsruhe began making horns and trumpets with "square" Stölzel-Blühmel valves. About this same time, modified "round" Stölzel-Blühmel valves were utilized on instruments produced by two Paris companies, Labbay and Halary. Many others soon followed suit. Sibyl Marcuse states that William Wieprecht and Johann Gottfried developed short piston valves of large diameter, known as *Berliner-Pumpen,* with two for the left hand and three for the right hand, all lowering the pitch of the open tones.[2] In 1824, John Shaw of England developed a transverse spring slide piston valve. In 1830, Leopold Uhlmann of Vienna developed a double piston valve known as the "Vienna valve." Until World War II most European horn players played double horns that utilized Vienna valves. Since that time, the majority of orchestral players have relinquished their Vienna valve horns in favor of the conventional rotary valve.

The rotary valve is commonly credited to European invention. However, David Hambelen claims that the rotary valve was invented in Lowell, Massachusetts, in 1824, by Nathan Adams of Milford, New Hampshire, some eight years before it was supposedly invented by J. Riedl of Vienna.[3] In his book *The Tuba Family,* Clifford Bevan also mentions Nathan Adams (1783–1864) as a musician, bandmaster, and instrument maker who developed a trumpet with three rotary valves connected by two wires to each rotor. "On the U.S. Frigate Constitution, in the Navy Yard at Charlestown, Mass., is a trumpet inscribed, 'Permutation Trumpet/Invented and Made by N. Adams, Lowell, Mass./Paul Heald, Caruske/Mass. 1825.'"[4] In 1832, in Vienna, Joseph Riedl's rad-machine was perhaps the first rotary valve with adjustable crooks and was thought of as a European phenomenon. The valve system known as the rotary valve on modern brass instruments is essentially the same as Riedl's creation.

Between 1835 and 1850, other makers in Berlin, Potsdam, Paris, Prague, and Vienna began to construct instruments with either Berliner-Pumpen or Vienna valves. During this same period, Adolph Sax of Brussels also copied the Berliner-Pumpen valves. Both of these valve mechanisms were later replaced by rotary valves, especially in Germany and Austria. In 1839, Pertinet of Paris brought out a piston valve that is still utilized in modern-day brass instruments. The Pertinet piston was a modification of the Berliner-Pumpen.

Mutual efforts of players and instrument makers to seek continual improvements in design and performance quality have brought about many experiments and innovations. The development of compensating valve systems providing for improved intonation is the result of such collaborations. Piston valve compensating systems started appearing during the 1850s, and today both piston and rotary compensating systems are important features on models of euphoniums and tubas produced by several instrument manufacturers. The compensating system endeavors to correct the iniquities of tubing length for various valve combinations, most specifically the 1-3 and 1-2-3 combinations. This is done by small additional lengths of tubing that are brought into use when the aforementioned valve combinations are used. Player adjustment of valve slides (crooks) continues to be an option for adjusting intonation. For this reason, many instruments have been designed to make the valve slides more accessible by placing them above the valve cluster. There are designs which place the main tuning slide above the valve. Individual tubists have a rod attachment placed on the main tuning slide (crook) extending below the valves. In either instance, the manipulation is done by the left hand. An important choice for compensating intonation is the addition of extra valves to the basic three-valve system. The addition of extra valves provides for extended low range and numerous alternate valve combinations giving the player intonation and response options.

The need for a bass brass instrument that could match the tone quality and dynamic range of the other brass instruments prompted many experiments by instrument makers throughout Europe and America during the early 1800s. Once the valve became a consideration, it was only a matter of time until their utilization would make possible a chromatic bass brass instrument. Such an instrument appeared in Berlin in the late 1820s. In 1828, Stölzel, co-inventor and co-pioneer of the valve, issued a price list of chromatic brass instruments including a bass horn or basstrompete in F or E-flat and a tenor horn or tenortrompete in B. These instruments were probably prototypes of the tuba and B-flat baritone. Models of these instruments were available in ophicleide or trumpet shape. In 1829, Wilhelm Wieprecht wrote marches for the Trompeton Corps of the Prussian Dragoon Guards, which included parts for these particular instruments. An early tuba was built in 1835 by Johann Gottfried Moritz and Wilhelm Wieprecht, most likely an alteration of the earlier Stölzel instrument.[5] Wieprecht was perhaps familiar with the single valved "ophicléide a piston," constructed by A. G. Guichard of Paris, a single-valved instrument that was an early form of the tuba in all but name. (On June 14, 1836, Guichard of France took out a five-year patent on the ophicléide a piston. He later developed a three-valved instrument.) Clifford Bevan makes it clear that

> there is only one instrument in the modern orchestra of which we know the precise date of birth: Prussian Patent 19 was taken out on 12 September 1835, by William Wieprecht and Johann Moritz of Berlin for the Bass-Tuba. The event was announced in a small paragraph on the front page of the "Allgemeine Precussische Staats-Zeitung" for Wednesday, 16 September 1835.[6]

Contrary to the above quote, conflicting data exists as to the precise origin and birthdate of the tuba. For example, it is known that Cerveny invented a contrabass tuba in 1834. The tuba jointly patented in 1835 by Weiprecht and Moritz was a bass tuba in F with five Berliner-Pumpen valves and was intended to replace the bass trombone. The Wieprecht-Moritz valves were short piston values of large diameter, known as Berliner-Pumpen, with two for the left hand and three for the right hand, all lowering the pitch of the open tones.

After the invention of the valves, the tuba family, from tenor to subcontra-bass, appeared in many shapes and sizes. This was true in fact of the entire brass family. By the mid-nineteenth century, the proliferation of bass wind instruments was of such great variety and configuration that some confusion of terms and nomenclature has existed to the present time. The bass horn, as used in a nineteenth-century context, usually referred to a woodwind instrument that was a variety of upright serpent in the general shape of a bassoon. The Russian bassoon was actually a nineteenth-century upright serpent with a brass bell. The word *bombardon* is generally accepted today as denoting a small tuba, but this was not always a consistent understanding in the nineteenth century. "Apparently, there were many hybrid models of so called tenor horns, euphoniums, and bombar-

ILLUSTRATION NO. 1

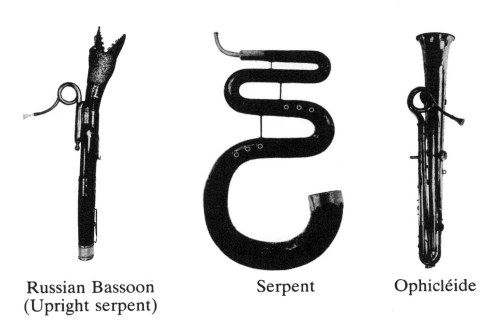

Russian Bassoon   Serpent   Ophicléide
(Upright serpent)

History of the Tuba and Related Instruments

dons which were called by various names from country to country with no standard nomenclature."[8]

The word *bombardon* possibly came from the bombardone of Italy. The "Italian bombardone" was the bass shawn, while the tenor shawn was simply named "bombarde." The shawns were early European ancestors of the oboe family and forerunners of the bassoon. The bombardon was called a "bass bombard" by Johann Riedl of Vienna, in reference to his twelve-keyed bass ophicleide invented in 1820. To circumvent the patent of a five-valve tuba by William Wieprecht and Johann Moritz, tuba makers referred to a tuba in F as a "bombardon." In 1845, Vaclav Cerveny, a Bohemian instrument maker, manufactured a six-valve tuba in F, which he called "bombard." A bombardon could also be a tuba in E-flat. In 1848, Hector Berlioz mentioned no less than seven basses of various kinds then in use: the ophicléide, bass in B, contrabass in F or E-flat, the bombardon in F, the German bass tuba, the old wood serpent, and the Russian bassoon.[9]

Robert E. Eliason, in his series of "A Pictorial History of the Tuba and Its Predecessors" in early *Tubist Universal Brotherhood Association* quarterly journals, reveals many curious designs: instruments that completely encircle the player's head and rest on both shoulders; over-the-shoulder models with the bell pointing to the rear or that have other unique features.

Terminology is extremely vague in dealing with the early tuba and related instruments. In 1838, Moritz patented a five-valve bass tuba in E-flat and four-valve tenor tubas. These tenor tubas were forerunners of the modern-day baritone and euphonium. According to Clifford Bevan, "the tenor tuba was superseded about 1843, by the Euphonium, invented by Konzertmeister Sommer of Weimer, apparently a tenor tuba with an even wider bore."[10]

Another forerunner to the modern-day baritone and euphonium was built in 1840, by Vaclav Cerveny. These instruments were called "Barytone or cor-basse tenor" in France, "barytonhorn" in Germany, and "baritono" in Spain.

References to the baritone horn and euphonium are often inconsistent and confusing. The length of the tubing of the two instruments is the same, and the range is parallel. However, the euphonium has a wider bore and (usually) a greater degree of taper. Also, the euphonium more often has a fourth valve and sometimes a fifth valve, which extends chromatic range down to the fundamental. For these reasons, the baritone voice is considered characteristic of the euphonium, while the tenor voice is more characteristic of the baritone horn. It is interesting to note that at the First International Tuba Symposium Workshop, held at Indiana University in 1973, the membership of Tubists' Universal Brotherhood Association (TUBA) officially adopted the name "euphonium" to replace the often-used nomenclature "tenor tuba" as referred to by Strauss in *Ein Heldenleiben* and *Don Quixote* and by Mahler in his Symphony No. 7. Modern-day euphoniumists are called upon to perform parts assigned by composers to the tenor tuba and are careful to separate their identity from that of the baritone horn or tenor tuba. Also, in the instrumentation of brass bands throughout the world, separate parts are played by the baritone horns and the euphoniums. Is important to note that while the euphonium (tenor tuba) did not gain a permanent place in the symphony orchestra, it rivaled the cornet as a "featured solo instrument" with Sousa and other great touring bands of the twentieth century.

Another important instrument of the tuba family developed in the mid-nineteenth century was the "Wagner tuba," or more correctly, the *Wagner Tuben*.* It was inspired by composer Richard Wagner. Wagner, a noted orchestrator of the era, showed a strong preference for four-voice choirs within the brass and woodwind sections of the orchestra. In his experiments of adding new colors to the orchestral body, he desired an instrument that would bridge the gap between the horn and the trombone. He contemplated a conical bore instrument that would extend the horn sound downward to the range of the trombone choir in the middle-low registers, thus creating the Wagner Tuben. In 1869, he utilized a section of these instruments in *The Ring of the Nibelung*. There has been a great deal of conjecture on the origin of this instrument. For example, "some leading authorities believe that Wagner probably heard an instrument called a *cornon* in Berlin in 1862 that satisfied the requirement for which he was searching."[11] The *Tuben* were in the keys of B-flat and F and were scored as a quartet. These instruments are usually played by horn players and are tubas in miniature, with wide tapers and a timbre very powerful and dark in character. The valves are arranged to be manipulated with the left hand. The Wagner Tuben have been used by only a few composers since the time of Wagner, most notably Bruckner, Mahler, Strauss, Holst, and Stravinsky. Since the Wagner Tuben are often not readily available, horns are substituted for them. Some major orchestras possess their own set of Wagner Tuben.

In 1834, Cerveny invented the contrabass tuba in BB-flat and CC. The shape of the instrument was in upright form (to be held in the lap of the player) or in circular form (to be held on the shoulder and referred to as the helicon). Sometime before 1845, a helicon was built in Russia and adopted by Russian bands. Bands of other European countries and the United States also adopted helicons. In 1848, Cerveny built a large-bore helicon, which was called "B-flat bass" in the United States and "tenorbass" in Germany. In 1849, Stowassen of Vienna also started producing helicons.

The upright tuba would later be known as "contrebasse a piston" or "tuba contrebasse" in France, "Kontra-bas" in Germany, and "tuba" or "basso tuba" in Italy. The Italian term *cimbasso* is traditionally applied to the lowest brass instrument in the orchestra, whether a bass trombone, contra-bass trombone, or tuba.

Perhaps the most important individual in correlating developments of various European instruments was Adolph Sax, a Belgian inventor and instrument maker. In 1843, Sax developed a series of valved bugles and patented them in Paris in 1845. These instruments were called "saxhorns." They had a medium conical bore, medium-sized bell, and were played with funnel-shaped mouthpieces. Sax erroneously claimed the invention of the valve bugle. Perhaps the most important contribution of Sax was his blending of related

*American musicians have anglicized the words tuben to become tubas and tube to become tuba.

The choice of rotary or piston valves is also a matter of personal preference. There are two basic types of piston valves: a standard length (preferred by most players) and a short-action valve intended to facilitate faster action. Several European manufacturers produce euphoniums and baritones with rotary valves. Whether rotary or piston, it is extremely important that valve parts align with the valve tubing.

Various intonation aids are featured on instruments available today. Automatic compensating systems are available on Besson (Boosey and Hawkes in Canada and England), Hirsbrunner, Willson, and Yamaha euphoniums. Other intonation aids provided by instrument manufacturers are a third-valve slide trigger (to adjust slide length) and a main tuning slide trigger (to adjust overall intonation). It is worth repeating that a fourth valve provides alternate combinations useful in correcting intonation on either a compensating or noncompensating instrument, especially the 1-3 and 1-2-3 combinations. A more detailed discussion of these considerations appears in chapter 5.

Early tubas were made without protective finish or lacquer. Modern tubas are available in a number of finishes including brass lacquer, brass epoxy lacquer, silver-nickel lacquer, and silver plating (at times with lacquer). Brass epoxy lacquer is the most durable lacquer and maintains its appearance best; however, many players prefer silver plating for appearance and playing quality. Others prefer a particular finish (or no finish at all) because they feel it enhances their tone.

Added features of more expensive instruments include extra bracing, protective sleeving (shield) along the outer pipe, and strong protective butt plates on the bottom bow. Good case construction offering maximum protection is also an important consideration. The sides and bell liner of the case should be well padded and reinforced, and the instrument should fit snugly.

Table 2.1.
Models of baritones (tenor horns) and euphoniums in use today.

Shape	Bore Size	Valves
upright	tenor horn (.504–.525)	piston 3
upright	baritone (.504–.579)	piston 3, rotary 4
upright	euphonium (.555–.651)	piston 4 to 5, rotary 4 to 5
bell-front	baritone (.562–.579)	piston 3
bell-front	euphonium (.562–.600)	piston 3 to 4
bugle (corps)	marching (.500)	piston 3
double bell	duplex	piston 5, rotary 5

Intonation Aids

compensating valves
valve trigger
rotary valve attachment to valve slide

Tuba

Tubas are available in a wide variety of models and designs. The particular models selected by an individual or music educator will depend on many factors. Educators must consider the needs of beginning band, marching band, concert band, orchestra, and other ensembles. They must also take into account the quality, durability, and price range permitted by their budgets. A single instrument that can be utilized for several ensemble situations is often an important determining consideration for the music educator. Where budgets permit, an educator may choose one type of instrument for the marching band (sousaphone or corps tuba) and another (professional-quality upright tuba) for the orchestra and concert band. When budgets are limited, educators may be wise to select convertible tubas (corps tuba) or tubas with interchangeable (upright and recording) bells. In the opinion of the authors, it is extremely important that every high school possess at least one professional-quality instrument for the players who demonstrate exceptional performance potential. Educators should also seek and consider the recommendations of professional artists. Professional players are generally much more concerned with the quality and the durability rather than with the cost. Professionals can also provide important guidance to the individual student and parents in the purchase of an instrument most suited to that individual.

A quality instrument, given good care, is one of the best investments one can make, for these instruments retain their value very well. Features to consider when selecting an instrument include design (configuration), bore size, bell size, finish, type of valves (rotary or piston; top or front action), number of valves, position of valves, and, most important, the response, tone quality, and intonation. It is good to note once again that professional players can provide invaluable guidance to students, parents, and music educators who are not themselves tubists.

Some instrument makers today offer models with three, four, five, six, and even seven valves; compensating valve systems; a choice of rotary or piston valves; thumb-operated valves; three or more bore sizes; plus various other special features that may give distinction to their particular products. For example, Besson offers large bore, four-valve tubas with compensating systems in CC and BB-flat; Meinl-Weston offers models with or without detachable bells; Mirafone produces many bore sizes in as many models, most of which are available in either CC or BB-flat with either four or five rotary valves; Cerveny provides several models of different sizes and configurations to a number of distributors; Rudolf Meinl produces both CC and BB-flat tubas in graded bore sizes; Yamaha markets rotary and piston valve instruments in various sizes; Besson, Conn, Deg, King, Yamaha, and others produce convertible (corps) tubas, in addition to their other models; Hirsbrunner of Switzerland and B & S have developed and marketed several new models in F, E-flat, CC, and BB-flat. The Peratucci company has worked with several tuba companies, developing special models and mouthpieces. The influence of determined and tenacious individual tubists, supported by the organized persuasion of TUBA, has brought about important collaborations between instrument makers and professional artists. These collaborations continue to effect changes and improvements. Suffice it to say, today's tubist has a large and varied collection of instruments from which to choose.

The following checklist of considerations should be of assistance to music educators and individual students in selecting an instrument for their personal use.

Appearance: Is the instrument well made? Is workmanship consistent and of high quality? Is it a good design, that is, does it please your eye and are the design proportions in balance? Do the basic shape, bore size, bell size, bell flare, valve layout, and valve type meet your established preferences and prejudices? If so, be prepared to put aside your prejudices as you give the instrument a proper testing and possibly discover that innovative design and unexpected playing qualities have given you a whole new set of personal preferences.

Inspection: Are there sufficient and well-placed braces to protect and strengthen the design? Does the instrument have protective shields (outer tubing) and butt plate (bottom bow)? Is the instrument well assembled (look for sloppy soldering of joints and braces)? Is the lacquer finish pitted, uneven, or discolored? Is the silver plating sufficient and even? Is the bell rim rolled or otherwise reinforced? Are the piston valves conveniently placed; that is, do they work quietly and smoothly without catching or binding? Can the instrument be held comfortably in playing position? Is the instrument well balanced? Can the valves be reached with relaxed arms, and without contorting the body position? Does the leadpipe placement meet your embouchure and allow you to have good body posture (not stretched or hunched over)? Can the upper valve slides be conveniently manipulated with the left hand?

Testing/Response: Does the instrument's response satisfy your concept of free-blowing and/or resistance (resistance to some is stuffiness to others). Does the instrument respond evenly throughout *your* range, or are some notes too stuffy and others too lively? Do alternate fingerings respond acceptably well (some alternates, especially 2-3, 1-4, 1-2-3, 2-4, 2-3-4, 1-3-4, and 1-2-3-4 combinations, will be more resistant than open notes or single-valve notes)? Uneven response is a serious drawback to any instrument. Check the fundamental (pedal tone) for easy response and full-tone quality. Often times a good pedal will indicate an instrument with excellent potential. A stuffy pedal is seldom found on a really fine instrument. Also, it is desirable to have some pitch variance on either side of the center of each pitch; this is important to playing in tune. Instruments that "lock in" pitches without variance are generally not desirable.

Intonation: Check intonation of the overtone series as follows:

1. open horn;

2. second valve;

3. first valve;

4. third valve/1-2 combination (compare: third valve is generally more in tune on European instruments);

5. 2-3 combination;

6. fourth valve/1-3 combination (compare: fourth valve is generally more in tune on European instruments);

7. 1-2-3/2-4 combinations (compare: 1-2-3 is traditionally very sharp, 2-4 is generally preferred);

8. all other combinations (see pages 54–57);

9. Give special consideration to the lower register (are the required combinations unnecessarily awkward? Also, can pitch adjustments be easily made by manipulating the upper-valve slides or main tuning slide?);

10. Do alternates and other tuning conveniences allow you to correct intonation faults of overtones? Bear in mind that these faults should be minimal.

Tone Quality: Are you pleased with the tone quality that you are able to produce on the instrument? Is the quality consistent throughout your range? Can tone quality be controlled at all dynamic levels? Are you able to modify tone quality (add high or low frequencies to brighten or darken sound)? If alternates are necessary for good intonation, is the tone quality consistent with conventional valve positions?

Flexibility: Does the combination of design, response, tone quality, intonation, and manipulations of same allow for maximum technical flexibility? Slurs across the overtone series should be manageable, and acoustical resistance (popping) from one valve combination to another should be minimal.

As of 1991, list price for a standard four-valve tuba of professional quality will vary from $1,800 to in excess of $12,000. This is quite a wide variance for initial cost. The wise purchaser will seek as much expert professional guidance as possible. Obviously, features offered by instruments in such a wide price range will vary greatly. Also, the purpose or ultimate use of the instrument is a prime consideration. It is also prudent to take resale value into account. None of the above-mentioned prices includes a trunk, hard case, or even a soft cover (gig bag). The availability and selection of these items is important for protecting the instrument. While the soft cover is primarily a "modesty cover" and offers minimum protection, it is most convenient for localized use. The trunk or hard case, on the other hand, is essential when traveling on any commercial transport and for storing the instrument. The instrument should fit snugly in a well-padded trunk or hard case, preferably one provided by the manufacturer or otherwise custom-made and of solid construction.

Table 2.2
Models of sousaphones and tubas in use today.

Shapes	Bore Size	Valves	
upright F	(.681–.728)	*piston 4,	rotary 4 to 6
upright E♭	(.572–.770)	*piston 3 to 5,	rotary 3 to 5
upright BB♭	(.610–.926)	*piston 3 to 4,	rotary 3 to 5
upright CC	(.675–.920)	*piston 4,	rotary 4 to 6
upright BB♭	(.630–.778)	*piston 3 to 4,	rotary 4 to 5
upright CC	(.675–.770)	*piston 3 to 4,	rotary 4 to 5
bell-front BB♭	(.710–.740)	piston 3 to 4,	rotary 4 to 5
bell-front CC	(.710–.740)	piston 4,	rotary 4 to 5

Intonation Aids

compensating valves
adjusting main tuning slide
adjusting 1st, 2nd, 3rd, 4th, and/or 5th valve slides
*(often 5th rotary valve with 4 piston valves or a
rotary valve attachment to valve slide)

In the latter part of the twentieth century there have been numerous changes in the quality, model variations, manufacturers, and distribution sources of music instruments (especially wind and brass instruments). It is therefore recommended that individuals or school officials contemplating the purchase of music instruments consult dependable sources of information as to current brands, models, and distributors. Local professional artists/teachers can provide invaluable assistance and recommendation. Local music dealers can also be helpful. Current listing of manufacturers, importers, and distributors of euphoniums and tubas should be available from TUBA.

The timbre or "core sound" produced on any instruments will vary greatly from one player to the next, depending on his concept of sound, his "musical voice," if you will. There are also personal opinions as to just what tonal characteristics are desirable for a given performance medium or, for that matter, a given composer. The timbre and quality of sound considered ideal for a quintet may not be the best choice for a symphony orchestra performance of, say, Wagner, Mahler, or Prokofiev. It is extremely important, therefore, that the individual performer not only seek instruments best suited to expressing his personal artistic concepts but also instruments that (in his opinion) best serve particular music disciplines. This is why many professional tubists own several instruments and never relax their search for yet a better instrument. The professional, serious student and music educator must consider every performance application: chamber ensemble (usually brass quintet), brass choir, wind ensemble, concert band, marching band, jazz combo, stage band, orchestra, solo/recital, and so forth. Obviously, in those many instances where a single instrument must serve a variety of ensembles, compromises must be made. However, such compromises can be kept to a minimum if an instrument is well chosen. As instrument companies produce more models and bore sizes, the quest of the professional for "the ideal instrument" will intensify, and the wise student and music educator will become increasingly dependent on the professional players' recommendations.

Instrument Evaluation Checklist for Advanced Performers

1. *Convenience, balance, and design appearance.* Can the valves and slides used for tuning be reached comfortably? In playing position, can you approach the mouthpiece without contorting your body, and does the instrument balance well (instruments without a good center of balance seem to fall away from the player)? Is it comfortable to sit with the instrument in playing position, without contortion and without stress?

2. *Response quality.* Does the instrument's blowing quality coincide with the player's attitude of "openness" or "resistance"? Is the instrument's response consistent throughout the player's range, taking into account all valve combinations?

3. *Dynamic qualities.* Is the tone quality and response acceptable throughout the player's range at all dynamic levels? Can pianissimos be controlled? Does the low register lose resonance, "crack," or "get edgy" when playing fortissimo?

4. *Intonation.* Taking into account that no instrument is perfect, can the intonation pattern of each valve combination (overtone series) be controlled and tuned? Can the diatonic and chromatic scale be played in tune without excessive mechanical or physical attention?

5. *Workmanship.* Is the instrument well made? Is it sufficiently braced? Are all joints sealed and braces neatly attached (no solder beads)? Are water keys easily accessible and properly located to fulfill their function? Is the finish (lacquer or plating) of good quality and appearance? Are the valves properly aligned? Are they solid or flimsy? Are they fast, quiet, and smooth working? Will they hold up to constant use?

6. *Purpose.* Will the instrument satisfy your requirements and intentions for use?

7. *Cost.* Is the instrument fairly priced? Is the instrument presented by a reputable firm? Is the sales representative known to be reliable and of good integrity? Will the instrument have good resale value if properly cared for?

8. *Aesthetics, preference, prejudice.* Does the instrument satisfy your concept of what other players suggest or are impressed with? Does it satisfy your prejudice for a particular valve system or configuration?

9. *Opinions, recommendations.* Have local artists/teachers been consulted for opinions and recommendations?

Chapter 3

TONE PRODUCTION, EMBOUCHURE, AND ARTICULATION

Good sound on any wind instrument is controlled primarily by the musical concepts and physical characteristics of the individual performer. The manner (speed and volume) in which the breath passes through the lips (embouchure) into the instrument, correct use of the diaphragm and abdominal muscles, openness of the throat, position of the throat, and formation of the mouth (oral cavity/resonating chamber), combined with embouchure shape and tension, produce and determine the quality of sound produced on brass instruments. Too often a well-meaning instructor, through verbose descriptions, will complicate the students' natural breathing process and inhibit rather than aid the students' progress. The natural process of breathing is simple. Once the student is using the breath and oral cavity correctly, he will be able to establish a proper concept of good tone quality. *At least 90 percent of tone production depends on air supply and support of the airstream. The embouchure, combined with breath control, provides the other 10 percent in refining and defining tone quality.* Through astute listening to teachers, other artists' live performances, and the many excellent recordings now available, the student through imitation can refine many performance skills. Critical to the development of tonal quality and tonal control is the study of songs, hymns, and melodic studies in cantabile style. Generally speaking, too little of a student's practice time is spent on melodic studies. It is extremely important that a well thought out and balanced program of technical and lyrical studies always be maintained!

The primary purpose of this chapter is to describe in simple terms those aspects of correct breathing that apply directly to tone production and good performance practice on brass instruments. We hope the chapter will offer a better understanding of correct breathing as it pertains to brass instrument performance.

Breathing as it Pertains to Brass Instrument Performance

Inhaling and exhaling air are the two parts of the breathing process natural and essential to the life of everyone. Breathing is done without thought. However, considerable thought regarding breath support and the breathing process are ongoing concerns and studies of every brass player. Early in their study of a brass instrument, students have impressed upon them the importance of knowing more about the breathing process. They learn that in addition to inhaling and exhaling air there are the additional considerations of containment and controlled release of air.

ILLUSTRATION NO. 2

Breathing Process

INHALATION   CONTAINMENT   EXHALATION

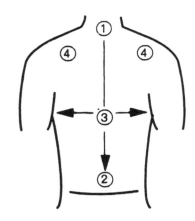 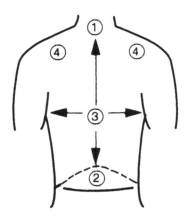 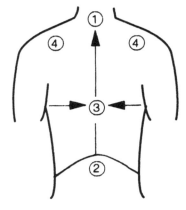

1. Inhale with open throat, filling lungs to capacity.
2. Contracting diaphragm assists intake of air.
3. Intake of air expands chest and upper torso. Muscles in torso area expand.

1. Glottis is used to contain air in lungs.
2. Diaphragm is contracted ("pushed down") by air capacity.
3. Chest and upper torso remain fully expanded.

1. Glottis is opened to control the release of air (without any muscle constriction in the area of the throat).
2. As pressure on contracted diaphragm is relieved by expulsion of air, the diaphragm gradually resumes normal position.
3. Chest and upper torso muscles contract (pulling in), forcing air out and increasing air pressure and velocity. Chest and upper torso reduce to normal, relaxed position.

4. Shoulders remain in normal, relaxed (unraised) position throughout inhalation, containment, and exhalation of air.
5. Control of the speed and amount of air inhaled, contained, and released is determined by demands of dynamics, tone quality, musical phrasing, and artistic interpretation as intellectually conceived and projected by the player.

Relaxed posture is essential to correct intake of air. Whether you are standing or seated, your shoulders and upper torso must be in normal relaxed positions and your throat "open." Air is taken in through an open throat to fill the lungs to capacity. As the lungs fill with air, the contraction of the diaphragm will assist inhalation; the diaphragm is "pushed down" (contracted) while the chest and entire upper torso is expanded by the intake of air.

Gradual return to relaxed posture is essential to correct expulsion of air. At the peak of lung capacity, the chest and entire upper torso is enlarged, and the muscles of this area are expanded. As air is exhaled—"pushed out" by compressing (pulling in) muscles in the area of the torso—the chest and entire torso become smaller and return to their original relaxed positions, ready for a new inhalation and expansion, another breath.

Movement of air into the lungs, then out (past and across the lips, causing the lips to vibrate and produce a given tone; into the mouthpiece and conceptually "through" the brass instrument) is often construed and represented as "one" exercise in "two" parts (inhale/exhale, breathe in/blow out). Also to be considered is the containment and controlled release of air as required by the demands of specific range, dynamic level, and note length. As air is released to start a tone (attack), a gentle rise occurs in the upper chest. This position is retained for the duration of the tone. If the upper chest drops at the time of initial attack, it indicates that the player is not properly utilizing full control of breath support. Illustration 2 displays the processes of inhalation, containment, and exhalation. The preceding narrative and examples demonstrate in a simple manner the process of correct breathing for brass players. To strengthen these examples the following three points are repeated:

1. Keep shoulders in normal, relaxed position *at all times*. Do not allow shoulders to raise during inhalation.

2. Always inhale with an "open" throat. Do not allow any constriction or tightness in the throat area during inhalation or exhalation.

3. For maximum expansions and control of inhalation, containment, and release of air, always keep the chest and upper torso in a normal erect position. Good posture is essential to correct breathing.

To further the potential for understanding every aspect of breath support and control, these additional concepts and information are provided.

Containment of air in the lungs is achieved by a natural closing of the glottis, thus preventing any escape of air from the lungs until the glottis is again opened. Containment of air in the lungs is usually for a brief time, although such containment may be prolonged in performance. It is important to avoid tension in the neck area, shoulders, and arms during this containment of air and to avoid air in the mouth (containing air with closed lips with open glottis), which may cause undesirable, explosive production of sound when released.

Exhalation is the third part of breathing. In wind-instrument playing this process takes the form of "blowing" and culminates in the exercise of breath support, breath control, and tone production. "Blowing" is accomplished by an inward, upward lifting of the

Tone Production, Embouchure, and Articulation

abdominal muscles. Depending upon one's physique, the chest may rise during the process. Activity employed by the abdominal muscles will depend on the amount of air projected to satisfy demands of range and/or dynamics. Further suggestions follow:

1. Without hesitation, fill up with air and blow; inhale and release; project the airstream.

2. Conserve and control the airstream at all times.

3. Practice the widest range of dynamics throughout your (personal) range.

4. Do not practice at the same dynamic level for long periods of time.

5. Keep the shoulders and chest relaxed when inhaling.

6. Avoid pulling your instrument into your body so firmly that it inhibits maximum expansion of the lungs.

7. Select an instrument you can comfortably handle with your physique.

8. Use an instrument stand or other support if necessary for good posture and comfort. Do not use an instrument stand that holds the instrument so rigidly and "immovable" that it causes you to adopt the bad habit of moving your head too much when changing registers. This can also choke off the flow of air. All instrument stands should allow flexibility for natural movements.

9. When inhaling, breathe to the bottom of the throat. Fill the lungs with air as you would a bucket of water, from the bottom up.

10. To experience lower outward expansion, try panting like a dog (slow the inhalation process and spread the expansive activity "all the way around your torso").

11. While sitting in a chair, bend at the waist and place your hands on the floor between your feet; try filling with air and note the feeling of rib cage expansion; now return to an upright position and repeat the exercise.

12. Lie down on a flat surface; relax completely; put your arms back over your head; deeply inhale and exhale.

13. For maximum deep breathing potential, always keep the midsection pliable. Never sit in a stiff or rigid upright position; always be relaxed and feel natural with your instrument in playing position.

Please note that the preceding suggestions cannot be accomplished with the shoulders and chest raised during inhalation. Remember, the worst enemies of proper breathing are tension and bad posture.

There are various musical studies and exercises for developing breath control; these include dynamic changes on long notes (crescendo–diminuendo—*ff*–*pp*; diminuendo–crescendo—*pp*–*ff* as well as long phrases in various vocal studies and etudes. Generally speaking, the approach to these studies is almost entirely concerned with utilizing full capacities of air and are invaluable to developing maximum breath control.

There are instances, however, particularly in articulated technical studies, when quick, small amounts of air are essential. The "hitch" breath and "sniff" breath are the two primary ways to quickly replace small amounts of air:

1. *Hitch breaths* are quick intakes of air through the mouth; usually (but not always) at the corners of the mouth, on one or both sides of the mouthpiece.

2. *Sniff breaths* are quick intakes of air through the nose, retaining embouchure position on the mouthpiece.

Both the hitch and sniff techniques are important to low brass players as alternatives to leaving out a note or cutting a note excessively short in order to take a full mouth breath.

"Circular breathing" is another technique that must be considered by all wind and brass players. Several published articles and books address circular breathing in lengthy detail. A simple definition here will perhaps inspire further investigation into this technique. Essentially, circular breathing is precisely a continuous "circular" supply of air, achieved by using the cheeks as a bellows (allowing them to fill with air from the lungs) and, while the facial (cheek) muscles are contracted to force controlled air through the lips to sustain sound, a fresh supply of air is taken through the nose and into the lungs to resupply the cheek bellows. Some players become so proficient at circular breathing that they are capable of sustaining a tone or phrase over several minutes. A few contemporary compositions now require circular breathing.

Hopefully, students will learn about correct breathing at the very beginning of their studies. Teachers should aid students' awareness by consistently checking their breathing and performance habits. *Correct breathing habits begin with good posture. All great brass teachers consider breathing to be the foundation and single most important aspect for developing good brass players.*

Breathing through the mouth while in playing position is best facilitated by dropping the lower jaw away from the mouthpiece and taking maximum air through an open throat into the lungs. Breathing through the corners of the mouth (on either side of the mouthpiece) can be effective, but is often a noisy interruption (especially when air is taken in fast or in large quantity).

When playing technical studies, it is helpful, to conserve and control the air and to avoid "gasping" for air, to think of blowing from the top half of the air supply. This concept helps to eliminate the problem of running out of air, swallowing excess saliva, or choking.

The basic embouchure for all brass instruments is essentially the same. Perhaps the simplest definition for a brass embouchure is a mouth with "firm corners," not tight corners, not corners pulled back, not corners pushed forward, but corners made firm where they naturally lie. The initial formation of the embouchure should be established in mid-range position in contact with the mouthpiece and with equal potential range development in both upward and downward directions. This should be a comfortable and natural feeling for the student, with firm controlled tension from all directions (similar to the lip formation achieved by pronouncing the syllable "too" or "pooh"). Stretching the lips (pulling back the corners of the mouth as when smiling) will cause a thin and "anemic" tone quality. Pushing the corners of the mouth forward ("puckering") will also restrict tone production and limit potential flexibility. Natural and comfortable

The Formation of the Embouchure

firmness of the corners without contorting will help establish a proper embouchure. A visual example to help demonstrate the feeling of proper jaw position and correct form for corners of the embouchure is to center a coin (nickel) flat between the lips, and hold the coin in that position for one minute (the coin must re main horizontal without tipping). This procedure may also be used as an endurance exercise (more about endurance exercises in chapter 4).

Placement of the mouthpiece on the mouth to best facilitate the forming of a proper embouchure is of extreme importance. Future bad habits can be avoided by careful and considered placement. Primary variables for locating the correct and most comfortable mouthpiece placement are basic shapes of lips, length of the upper lip, and formation of teeth. The natural embouchure "opening" for most players can be determined by producing a lip "buzz" without a mouthpiece (or with a mouthpiece "ring"). This natural embouchure opening position may be influenced by facial structure, teeth formation, size and shape of the mouth, and balanced or unbalanced muscular strength on either side of the mouth. For maximum potential development, it is always best to center mouthpiece placement on the natural embouchure opening. It is wise to avoid extremes and to note that any off-center variation of the natural embouchure opening is usually only 1/16 to 1/18 of an inch.

Equally important to left-right mouthpiece placement is consideration of upper-lower placement. It is well to note that the great majority of successful low brass players utilize a mouthpiece placement of approximately 60 percent upper lip and 40 percent lower lip. Seldom are superior results achieved when more mouthpiece is placed on the lower lip. Perhaps this is because the upper lip serves as a constant (retains basic shape, regardless of range, and changes tension minimally, except in extreme upper range), while the lower lip serves as a variable (changing in shape, thickness, and tension:

ILLUSTRATION NO. 3

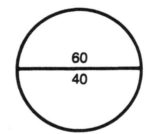

ILLUSTRATION NO. 4

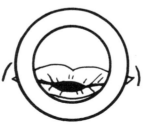   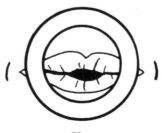   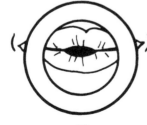

No   Yes   No

Please note: The opening in the lips is caused by moving air stream

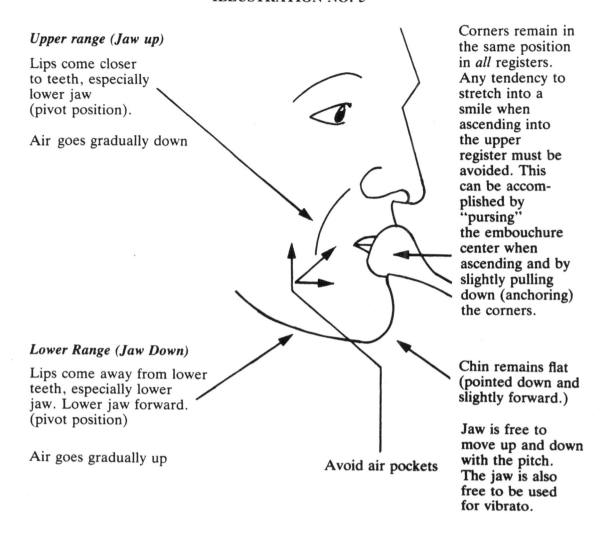

Upper range (Jaw up)

Lips come closer to teeth, especially lower jaw (pivot position).

Air goes gradually down

Corners remain in the same position in *all* registers. Any tendency to stretch into a smile when ascending into the upper register must be avoided. This can be accomplished by "pursing" the embouchure center when ascending and by slightly pulling down (anchoring) the corners.

Lower Range (Jaw Down)

Lips come away from lower teeth, especially lower jaw. Lower jaw forward. (pivot position)

Air goes gradually up

Chin remains flat (pointed down and slightly forward.)

Jaw is free to move up and down with the pitch. The jaw is also free to be used for vibrato.

Avoid air pockets

larger, thicker, and looser when approaching the low register and thinner, and tauter when approaching the upper register). Flexible movement of the lower jaw from one register to another is facilitated by keeping the upper rim of the mouthpiece "anchored" on the upper lip. The lower jaw drops or raises to accommodate changing thickness of the lower lip and the size of the oral cavity ("resonating chamber" of tone production). Illustrations 3, 4, and 5 provide graphic displays of mouthpiece placement utilized by the majority of low brass instrumentalists, particularly euphonium and tuba players.

Study illustration 5 carefully. Take into consideration the following:

1. Firm (not tight) corners of the mouth (embouchure) remain in the same position throughout the developed and potential range of the individual player. The corners must be "anchored" in place. *Avoid any tendency to pull back the corners when ascending into the upper register. Resist the tendency to "puff" cheeks when descending into the low register.*

Tone Production, Embouchure, and Articulation

2. Chin remains flat, pointed down, and brought slightly forward.

3. In the middle register the upper and lower teeth are generally in alignment and slightly parted; lips remain in contact until air passes through them, causing them to vibrate and create the natural embouchure opening. The lower jaw remains in a relaxed natural/neutral position. Upper rim of the mouthpiece remains in place, corners of the embouchure remain "anchored" in place.

4. The low register is approached by gradually dropping the lower jaw, keeping lips together (note how the lower lip increases in size/thickness as the lower teeth are pulled down by the dropping jaw and chin; note also that the inside of the mouth—oral cavity and resonating chamber—becomes larger, accommodating resonance of the lower tones). Upper rim of the mouthpiece remains in place, corners of the embouchure remain "anchored" in place. The instrument is "tilted" back slightly to accommodate dropping the lower jaw. *Avoid any tendency to "puff" cheeks.*

5. The upper register is approached (from the middle register neutral position) by gradually raising the lower jaw, keeping lips together, gradually adding tension to the embouchure by "pursing" toward the center of the embouchure, and gently pulling down (anchoring/strengthening) the corners of the embouchure. These coordinated actions will cause lips to have tighter contact with the teeth (especially the lower teeth) and decrease the size of the oral cavity/resonating chamber, thus accommodating resonance of the upper register tones. The instrument is "tilted" forward slightly to accommodate raising the lower jaw. *Avoid any tendency to pull back the corners when ascending into the upper register.*

6. Keep an open throat at all times, in all registers.

7. Note that the direction of the airstream changes slightly from one register to another: middle register—airstream directed forward, straight ahead; lower register—airstream directed gradually upward; upper register—airstream directed gradually downward.

8. Embouchure strength must be established and confirmed in the middle register *before* exploration of extreme ranges, especially the upper range. Gradual development of extended range will assure maximum endurance and *one* embouchure for the entire potential range. Gradual development of extended range will also help avoid bad habits of too much pressure, "register breaks" (a separate embouchure for middle/low/high registers), and facial contortions (puffed cheeks, flabby embouchure, etc.).

9. As mentioned earlier, the syllable of "too" or "toe" is ideal for producing tone and developing initial strength in the middle register.

Establishment of a proper embouchure is fundamental to every brass player's development. After breath support and breath control, a proper embouchure is the next most important consideration for every brass instrumentalist. It is the responsibility of every teacher to ascertain correct understanding and steady development of each student's basic equipment, both mental and physical: attitude, commitment, talent, health, breath support, breath control, embouchure, tone, articulations, overall technique, musical growth, and artistic potential. Remember, good habits never have to be broken. Valuable time is wasted when lesson and practice time is spent trying to overcome bad habits or bad attitude.

Student–Teacher Checklist

BREATHING/POSTURE

Breathing must be unrestricted. Good posture is essential.

Sit erect (not rigid), upper torso relaxed, shoulders relaxed (down), midsection pliable, instrument balanced, mouthpiece placed correctly, naturally, and comfortably (the instrument becomes an extension of the player), fingers on respective valves at all times, feet flat on the floor.

Stand erect (not rigid); see above comments.

Use instrument stand or other support if it aids free breathing.

Inhale with an open throat. Fill lungs with air like you would a bucket with water, from the bottom up.

Control containment and release of air. Airstream direction and velocity controlled to meet demands of pitch and dynamic.

EMBOUCHURE

Mouthpiece placed correctly and comfortably.

Embouchure formed without distortion; flat chin pointed down, firm corners in natural/neutral position, not pulled back, not pushed forward.

No air between lips and teeth (no air pockets).

Tongue down in a relaxed out-of-the-way position.

Concentrate on pitch relationship: lower lip is variable in shape, thickness, and tension; upper lip is constant in shape, with minimum variation of tension (except in extreme upper register).

Lower jaw slightly forward (teeth aligned) for basic mid-register embouchure.

Concentrate on pitch relationship: lower jaw moves in the direction of the pitch (down for low register, up for upper register); airstream is directed opposite to lower jaw movement (airstream up for low register, down for upper register).

Articulation

It is musically imperative that all brass artists develop articulations of every possible variety by utilizing all the vowels and consonants that have musical application to the communicative art of music. Most method books and pedagogical treatises limit themselves to the presentation of the single tongue ("attack") articulation. Generally the recommendation is to pronounce the syllable "tu" or "too" for commencing a tone and properly applying the use of the tongue. This approach is excellent as far as it goes, but seldom is it pointed out that other ("vocal") vowel syllables are also important to consider: "ee," "oh," "uh," "ah"; "tee," "toe," "tuh," "tah"; "dee," "doe," "duh," "dah"; "kee," "koe," "kuh," "kah"; "ghee," "go," "guh," "gah"; "thee," "tho," "thu," "tha"; "he," "hoe," "huh," "hah," and so forth are all valid, useful, and applicable in expressive artistic music interpretation. Such sophisticated elaboration of articulation possibilities might be too much for the beginner to cope with, but at some point in the advanced training of a student these possibilities should be introduced. The variety of articulation elaborations should be presented to each student only after he has mastered a good tone quality and a solid dependable single "too" articulation. It is quite easy for most students to immediately understand and accept the benefits of good tone production afforded by the use of "ah" in the low register, "ee" in the upper registers, and "ou" or "oh" in the middle, upper, and lower registers. The total range of subtleties achieved with the various articulation and use of vowels is limited only by each individual's concepts. It is the authors' belief that the tuba and euphonium are more "vocal" than "metal" and thus endorse the concept of "vocalizing" scales and arpeggios in much the same way as a singer vocalizes.

While discussing articulations (note beginnings—attacks, if you will), it is appropriate to mention the importance of releasing (ending) notes musically. Techniques for ending notes are seldom mentioned in method books or alluded to by many teachers. Often the primary differences in artistic refinement between one performer and another is the manner of note releases. Simply stated, the cleanest release of a note (or tone) is to cease the projection of air (without closing the throat, mouth, or lips and without cutting off the air with the tongue), allowing the tone to end, projected, tapered, and unrestricted. There are of course other ways to end notes, and each of the many alternatives (throat, tongue, lips, valve, etc.) has stylistic, interpretive musical applications.

In the performance of certain avant-garde contemporary compositions and in the performance of the varying stylistic disciplines of jazz composition, the subtle (sometimes not so subtle) use of vowels and articulations (beginning and release, "double-tonguing," shapes, fall-offs, doits, bends, varying vibrato width and speed, etc.) is often essential to authentic interpretation; just as the absence of such a myriad of techniques is essential to the authentic interpretation of baroque, classical, and romantic literature. The musician who places limits on the techniques he is willing and/or able to master is a limited interpreter of the musical arts. Indeed, there is one language of music, but there are many dialects. To be fully conversant in this language one must master the "regional" vocabulary, grammar, inflection, and pronunciation of each dialect and, in this context, be conversant in every music discipline. In conclusion, it is once again a matter of techniques serving the music and (hopefully) not the reverse.

Many artistic performers are bothered by the tone production and harsh, explosive attacks used by some students and colleagues. *The reasons brass players develop harsh, explosive attacks and bad tonguing habits are as follows:*

1. Breath support is not sufficient. (Every articulation should be at least 90 percent air.)

2. The lip has not developed sufficient flexibility to respond to the correct action of the tongue. Therefore, much of the difficulty in articulating musically is not because of the tongue but because of the lip. The lip can be strengthened by conscientious daily practice of lip slurs and flexibility studies (with proper breath support).

3. There is too much mouthpiece pressure on the lip, constricting responsiveness of lip tissue. One solution to this problem is to use more air (breath support!).

Some common problems are as follows:

1. Having the tongue act as piston. Too many players try to drive the air into the instrument with the tongue. *The correct action of the tongue is serving as a valve to release the air.*

2. Tonguing between the lips. Though advocated by Arban in his *Complete Method for Cornet and Trumpet* and endorsed by a few professional artists, it is the opinion of the authors that this technique of tonguing in the middle and upper ranges creates many problems for low brass players. Such articulations lack subtlety or refinement and are too heavy. However, the technique of tonguing between the lips can sometimes be helpful in the extreme low (pedal) register.

It is important to have the tongue articulation *in front* of the released air. An indication that the player is not properly using his tongue to start the tone is the hissing sound of escaping air preceding the production of musical sound.

The function of the tongue is to assist the air and embouchure in producing clean articulations. This consists of embouchure preparation, projection of the air stream, and application of the tongue, coordinated with precision. Following are some suggested articulations along with exercises considered valuable to improving the articulation:

1. Articulate each note without any tongue action at all, "ho," "ho," and so forth. This will assure breath support for each tone and impress on the student that breath is the most important factor in starting and controlling the length of each tone.

2. Articulate each note with the syllables "kee"/"ku" ("ghee"/"gu"), using the back of the tongue (articulate the syllable).

3. Alternate "tu" and "ku" (double tongue), striving to make them of equal accent and length.

4. The accepted "correct" Arban triple tongue utilizes the syllables of "tu-tu-ku" ("du-du-gu").

5. Other articulations that must also be mastered are the syllables "tu-ku-tu" and "ku-tu-ku," which simply alternate the accepted syllables for double and triple tonguing. In some passages this method often proves to be more satisfactory for speed and evenness than "tu-tu-ku." The various articulations should become part on one's daily routine of scales and arpeggios; one shouldn't perform articulations just on one repeated note. Double and triple

tonguing "tu-ku-tu-ku" are required techniques for all brass players.

6. The different disciplines of traditional and modern music literature demand that brass players be proficient in articulations of jazz (fall-offs, doits, bends, shakes, variable speed and width of vibrato, growls, etc.) as well as double stops, multiphonics, flutter tongue, and so on. Articulation can be improved by adhering to a daily routine that includes basic principles of various brass instrument articulations. With practice and experience, the player should be able to artistically shape tones and achieve infinite tonal colors necessary for musically expressive performances in any style.

Table 3.1 shows the relationships of main areas pertaining to tone production: air, embouchure, tongue/jaw, and variables.

Table 3.1

Tone Production

GOALS	AIR	EMBOUCHURE	TONGUE & JAW	OTHER
Centered Sound	Correct procedures	Corners firm	"Dead" tongue Drop jaw	Good concept of sound
Upper Range	More compression Air stream pointed down	Corners in control Pivot system	Teeth close together; still spaced and jaw pointed	Lips come closer to teeth
Lower Range	Replaced flow of air	Corners in control Pivot system	Jaw dropped & still pointed Teeth slightly parted	Lips relax from teeth
Endurance	Very important (90%)	Reduce work to as few muscles as necessary Minimum pressure at all times	Relaxed	Matter of pacing oneself
Intonation (the ear)	Consistent	Consistent	Consistent	Slide position four or more valves
Initial Attack	Right behind tongue (do not hold air behind tongue)	No excessive pressure	Drop tongue once articulation is made	
Contrast *ppp-fff*	Firmer abdominal wall for *ff* Resistance varies with instrument types	*ppp* more control in relaxed setting		Bell direction effects volume
Intervalic Flexibility	Directed flow of air —take more than planned to use Controlled support	Corners firm	Jaw goes in direction of pitch	
Technique and Speed	Air—(90%) Embouchure tongue (10%)	Corners firm	Coordination of tongue/fingers/ air Isolation of jaw	Avoid practicing mistakes
Warm-up (Warm-down)	Air (90%)	Corners firm Concept understood	Consistent	Use mirror— Be alert! Listen carefully
Other				Condition of instrument

COORDINATION: For clearly articulated tones, the air, tongue, embouchure, and fingers must be coordinated together. Equal consideration must be given to each of these factors if they are to work in unison. Should problems of coordination be suspect, standard exercises may be articulated without the instrument at varying tempos and under close observation. The player (or teacher) may then identify and correct coordination problems.

FUNCTION OF THE LIPS: The lips influence and define the pitch of each tone. They must therefore be positioned and shaped to produce the desired pitch with clear, tongued articulation. If the lips are buzzing a sound other than the desired predetermined pitch, a tone may be tongued flawlessly and still not be clear.

One test to determine if the lips are causing poor articulations is to play a tone several times in a row; if the sound becomes cleaner with repetition, it indicates that the lips were not initially set and focused properly.

HEARING AND VIBRATING CORRECT PITCH: The ear must hear the correct pitch for the mind to direct proper formation of the lips. The ear demands that correct pitch be maintained and that the lips be shaped to produce that pitch.

Another test of proper lip formation is to buzz the lips without the mouthpiece and produce a predetermined pitch, add the mouthpiece (retaining pitch), then add the instrument (still retaining pitch). This procedure is excellent ear (and embouchure) training and will help to identify incorrect buzzing of pitches.

Correct lip vibrations will not only help eliminate poor articulations, often blamed on the tongue, but will also benefit tone quality and the control and refinement of intonation.

BASIC POSITION OF THE TONGUE: The correct basic mid-range position of the tongue can most easily be determined by pronunciation of the syllables "too" or "toe." Gradual adjustments of this position will occur as articulations and clarity of tone are pursued throughout the complete range of one's instrument. Variations of the basic and altering position of the tongue for upper and lower ranges will be influenced to varying degrees by the length and shape of an individual's tongue, the size and shape of his mouth (oral cavity), and his teeth formation.

MOVEMENT OF THE TONGUE: Controversy exists among brass players as to which direction the tongue should move for articulations ("in-out" or "up-down"). Advocates of each approach have claimed success with their students. The authors suggest individual experimentation with both approaches but favor the up-down approach overall. (The

Tone Production, Embouchure, and Articulation

in-out approach may be used with success in the extreme low register of the euphonium and tuba).

The concept of the up-down technique is described as anchoring the tip of the tongue back of the lower teeth allowing the middle portion of the tongue to rise up and dent, interrupt, or break the air stream, then return to its original position, ready for another action upward. It is convenient to think of this procedure as that of a knife moving up and down, cutting the long horizontal air stream into segments or lengths of written notation.

VOWEL SOUNDS AND THE ORAL CAVITY: The different vowel sounds, their shaping, and pronunciation are defined and refined by the position and action of the tongue in the mouth (oral cavity). The oral cavity serves as the resonating chamber for brass instruments. The slightest alteration of the oral cavity's size and shape is effected by movement of the tongue and/or lower jaw. Alterations of the tongue position (even on a repeated tone) become quite obvious (and necessary) when double or triple tonguing. Also, be aware that the most subtle adjustment of intonation (and blend) is a change of color/timbre effected by changing vowel sounds and not an actual change of pitch (more about intonation in chapter 4).

REGISTER CHANGES AND THE ORAL CAVITY: As the oral cavity and embouchure are adjusted to accommodate the low register, the tongue stays with the lower jaw and rests lower in the mouth. As the jaw is raised and embouchure adjustments made for the upper register, the tongue moves up with the jaw and the oral cavity becomes smaller. However, especially with euphonium and tuba, the tongue is never positioned "high" in the oral cavity, even in the upper register. To do so restricts the flow of air, impedes proper shaping of the oral cavity and results in a thin, pinched-sounding tone quality.

EXCESSIVE JAW MOVEMENT: Excessive movement of the lower jaw, or "chewing" articulation, is a common fault to be avoided. While the jaw must be free to gradually open (lower register) and close (upper register), there should not be movement of the jaw for every tongued articulation. The use of a mirror during practice times will help players to avoid excess jaw motion (chewing articulations) as well as other bad habits of embouchure and posture ("seeing yourself as others see you," so to speak).

TONGUING THROUGH THE LIPS: Tonguing through the lips is generally to be avoided on euphonium and tuba, though in the extreme low register the technique may be useful or even necessary with some players. For clarity and speed in the extreme upper register, very short strokes of the tongue work best.

DETERMINING PROPER TONGUE USAGE: For most of the range of euphonium and tuba a good rule is to utilize the minimum amount and motion of the tongue to achieve maximum desired results. It should be noted that when making soft articulations the tongue is soft and pliable, and less tongue motion is used. Loud articulations are made with a firmer tongue and with slightly more motion. In general, a relaxed tongue will facilitate articulations and thus technical flexibility and speed. Ultimately, each individual must (with the guidance of good teaching) sort out for himself the best (most natural) tongue placement for all registers.

TONE PRODUCTION AND ARTICULATIONS: As stated in the first paragraph of this chapter, tone production (including any type of articulation) is at least 90 percent air (and support of the air stream). This percentage ratio allows 10 percent consideration for the shaping and pronunciation of each tone, inclusive of oral cavity shaping (resonating chamber), tongue position and action (articulation), lip/embouchure preparation (buzzing/vibrations of pitch), mouthpiece placement (contact and position), and finger selection of appropriate valve(s). Needless to say, elements of this 10 percent consideration must be well trained and coordinated.

BREATH ARTICULATIONS: The use and refinement of "breath articulations" deserves added attention and consideration. With breath articulations the ratio becomes 96 percent air and 4 percent oral cavity, embouchure, mouthpiece, and valves (the tongue simply lies in the mouth, staying out of the way except when shaping a vowel sound or otherwise altering the oral cavity). Mastering variations of the breath articulation, at all dynamics and in all registers, is of major importance. The breath articulation allows a note to commence without percussive beginning, to start from "nothing." It allows for large articulated skips from one register to another without space between. It is the basis for performing with "breath control," a refined addition to breath support, and the essential element for eliminating unwanted, interfering sounds of valves changing from one combination to another as they cross over from one overtone series to another. Every note within a slurred phrase is (ideally) a breath articulation (not a valve or tongue articulation). The breath articulation is the preferred articulation in the extreme low register, a viable alternative to tonguing through the lips. Indeed, "control" of the breath for the beginning, duration, and ending of each tone is artistic perfection to be sought after at all times. Yes, there can be breath support without breath control; there cannot be breath control without breath support. It is the authors' opinion that an infinity of articulations are possible, desirable, and invaluable to musical expression on the brass instruments. In addition to well-chosen, well-placed and appropriate vibrato ("none" is better than "too much") at the right speed and width, the choices of articulation determine the proper stylistic nuance and interpretation of every piece of music performed.

CONDITIONED REFLEX AND MUSICAL LOGIC: Every articulation (whether breath or tongue) ultimately has to be a "conditioned reflex" rendered instantaneously by the player's mental image of how he wants a given note or passage to sound—what impression or message he wishes to present to an audience. Bear in mind that all elements of a performance are finally judged by the tone quality, accuracy, technique, flexibility, and musical message produced by the performer. Giving the content of this treatise and others every consideration, it is recommended that the old saying, "It's what comes out the bell that matters," be constantly, seriously, and faithfully observed by all brass players. Think about it; if it isn't logical, it will probably not be musical.

Chapter 4

DEVELOPING AND MAINTAINING PERFORMING SKILLS

The achievement of maximum technique and lip flexibility in all registers is a major concern of every serious brass player. To accomplish this lifetime pursuit requires many hours of organized and dedicated practice. It is unfortunate that too many aspiring (and dedicated) brass players never come close to their flexibility potential simply because their approach to achieving this important goal is not well organized and often times misdirected. A balanced program of progressive studies covering all aspects of brass performance is essential to mastering any instrument, but remember that before you master your instrument you must first be a slave to it.

Daily practice will bear rewards commensurate to the planning and organized investment of time. Self-evaluation in private practice should be regularly reviewed with master teachers and observed in comparison with one's peers. For beginners and intermediates, progress is always most productive and rewarding under the guidance of a good teacher. Also, at these first two levels care should be taken to solidly master basics of tone production and control, articulations and dynamics, scales and arpeggios. It is recommended that every wind player also study piano and theory and that they listen to both live and recorded performances of accomplished players on their respective instruments. Knowing the literature and performance standards for one's instrument is a prerequisite to intelligent and inspired study.

Young players should be cautious about jumping too far ahead of their level of accomplishment and should heed the counsel of knowledgeable teachers who encourage and constantly challenge them. Harmful results and entrenched, hard to overcome, bad habits can result from reckless pursuit of extreme registers and dynamics not yet fully developed. Essential to orderly development is early understanding and adoption of a sensible warm-up and daily routine in balance with a player's level of development. Students able to extend their practice time to four or more hours a day and advanced/professional players who regularly play six to nine hours daily may wish to consider the benefits of a warm-down routine, done at the end of each work day. The endless quest for an ever more beautiful tone, increased range, technical flexibility, and masterful control of all aspects of instrumental performance should be exciting, inspiring, and rewarding. Without direction and organized self-discipline it can be boring and counter-productive. Don't let this happen to you. To a dedicated musician a career in music is not a matter of life and death; it is far more important than that.

Warm-Up Purpose and Definition

The primary purpose of a warm-up routine is to assure oneself that skills already mastered are available for use in an impending practice session or performance, skills like a full and pleasing tone, dynamic control, varying articulations, lip slurs up and down, extended range, arpeggios and octaves, scales, rhythmic patterns, and melodic embellishments. A brass warm-up can be of any length (five minutes or more) and should always commence in the middle register. Active advanced/professional performers (six to nine playing hours per day) generally will not require a lengthy warm-up (though they may wish to also consider a warm-down) for they are assuring themselves of skill-retention through constant application. However, if the types of performance disciplines in which these players are active do not demand a full range of instrumental skills, unused skills must be included in their warm-up (or daily routine). The inactive or occasional player, say one who performs only on weekends or less often, not only needs a longer warm-up but also a very disciplined one to avoid possible injury to the embouchure and "to save something" for that weekend performance.

Students and players at every level should always warm up before each practice, rehearsal, or performance; even before they apply themselves to their daily routine. Such self-imposed discipline will pay dividends throughout their life in music. Teachers should assist each student in tailoring a personalized warm-up that suits his individual level. The student will be rewarded and reminded of his progress as new skills are added to his warm-up.

Every warm-up should start with whole notes in the mid-range at moderate (p–mf) dynamics and gradually extend into the upper and lower range by both single articulations and legato phrasing. Next, scales and arpeggios (both slurred and articulated) can be added, followed by progressive and extended-interval lip slurs and flexibility exercises. Loud dynamics and extreme registers (especially the high) should not be explored until the player's embouchure is relaxed, pliable, and strong. The warm-up will stimulate the flow of blood through the tissue of the lips and help establish basic embouchure for more adventuresome playing such as a player's personal daily routine. A faulty, inconsistent embouchure is often the result of starting to play "cold" without warm-up. Accuracy of note placement is directly related to consistency of embouchure throughout one's complete range; proper warm-up is a definite factor.

Every warm-up (warm-down) should include intelligent application of both the mental and physical considerations of brass instrument playing. Concentration regarding musical and technical goals must be directed toward applying the physical requirements of breath (support/control), embouchure (mouthpiece placement), tongue/jaw (position/range), and coordination of muscles controlling the fingers (valve technique). All these factors must be controlled and evaluated by each individual's artistic taste and musical "conditioning." A teacher's guidance plus the "learning environment" of the student are the two most significant influences in developing the student's ability to judge himself as well as others; together, these factors mold the student's musical opinions and taste. A warm-up (at whatever level) should assure the player's readiness for the daily routine, practice session, or impending rehearsal or performance. A warm-up should leave the player relaxed, alert, and confident about his ability.

Warm-Down Purpose and Definition

As mentioned above, a warm-down routine should be of interest to players who regularly perform four or more hours each day. Warming down is quite similar to warming up, though perhaps of shorter duration and in reverse order. That is to say, ending with long tones in the middle register and at soft dynamic levels. As is the case with a warm-up, a warm-down should leave the player relaxed and satisfied about his performance. A thoughtful and concentrated warm-down can help prevent stiffness in the embouchure, an undesirable condition to experience ("the morning after"). Again, players are encouraged, and expected to be self-motivated and self-reliant about their own well-being. A warm-down takes little time and may just save tomorrow for the prudent brass player.

Daily Routine: Purpose and Definition

Every player should adopt a daily routine that covers all basic instrumental techniques, tonal studies, scales, arpeggios, extended range, slurs, lip flexibility studies, and so forth. The "daily routine" can be thought of as an extended and adventuresome warm-up. It should both assure and challenge the player. It should remind the player of skills that need further improvement in the practice room. Each player should customize his daily routine to encompass the special demands of his particular performance career goals. Rhythmic and melodic patterns, special exercises of difficult coordination, lip trills, and overtone rips (both up and down) are a few special techniques that might be added to a standard daily routine. It is important to remember that a daily routine is not a replacement for practice time but rather daily "insurance coverage" for acquired skills. New skills will still need to be explored, developed, and perfected in the practice room. The daily routine can be (should be) regarded as a daily self re-evaluation, as important to continued performance health as the daily brushing of one's teeth is to dental hygiene.

Practice

Other than the preparation and presentation of public performances, the single most important activity for instrumentalists is *practice.* More than any other consideration, practice ultimately determines the level of performance success achieved by any musician. Talent will assist and enhance artistic development, but it is *time* that makes it possible; time spent studying and practicing and time putting into practice the skills developed and refined. Study with a master teacher is extremely important, but the benefit of a one-hour private lesson each week must be extended by a minimum of twenty-eight hours of practice (four hours each of seven days a week), *not* rehearsing and *not* performing but *practicing.* The master teacher is compensated for his valuable time minimally for each contact hour and maximally by the number of hours each of his students practice. The student is rewarded for each practice hour with personal growth, artistic achievement, and ultimately by a career in music as a performer.

Throughout warm-up, practice, rehearsal, and performance, one must maintain a consistent attitude, awareness, and concern for quality, accuracy, control, and musicianship (quality tone and articulations, accurate placement of pitch and intonation, control of dynamics, and a balanced ensemble blend with other instruments).

Warm-Up Considerations for Euphonium and Tuba

Provided below is an outline of points to consider in creating or evaluating a warm-up.

I. Mental
   A. Rethink your commitment to music and your instrument.
   B. Consider your state of mind and body; relax. Take into account whether you are fresh and alert or tired and disoriented.
   C. Review the purpose of your warm-up and your schedule for the day.
   D. Resolve to focus full attention and concentration on your warm-up routine.
   E. *Check out the following physical considerations before each warm-up until they become automatic—conditioned reflex.*

II. Physical
   A. Good posture (seated and standing)
   B. Embouchure setting
      1. Mouthpiece placement
      2. Firm corners
      3. Relaxed jaw
(The use of a full length mirror is recommended to verify these points and to avoid facial contortions and the development of any bad habits related to the embouchure. Every student should have a small practice mirror. It is recommended that the practice room and teaching studio be equipped with full-length mirrors.)
   C. Breathing
      1. Relaxed upper torso. Take several deep breaths and slowly inhale-exhale. Be assured of comfortable "free" breathing.
      2. Taking a breath. Fill lungs to capacity. Shoulders should be in normal relaxed position (not raised).

III. Technical
   A. Tone production (response)
   B. Articulation (attacks and releases)

   C. Flexibility (lip slurs)

   D. Range (scales, arpeggios)

   E. Technique (speed, clarity)—use of metronome is recommended.

IV. Musical

   A. Tone quality (crescendo/diminuendo)

   B. Intonation (arpeggios, scales)

   C. Rhythm (subdivision)—use of metronome is recommended.

   D. Interpretation (phrasing, style)—use of tape recorder is recommended.

V. Warm-up goals

   A. Preparation. Be assured that all developed skills are performance-ready and can be applied to the immediate purpose (practice, rehearsal, performance).

   B. Endurance. Be assured that mental and physical considerations are unrestricted by either lack of concentration or bad playing habits that will sap strength needed for maximum endurance.

VI. Proceed with warm-up

The following illustrations provide examples of the types of exercises one may wish to incorporate in formulating a personal warm-up routine.

Warm-Up and Daily Routine for Euphonium and Tuba

I.   Check list for warm-up (mental and physical)

   A. Use correct breath support (use full-length mirror).

   B. Use correct embouchure in all registers (use mirror to check corners).

   C. Increase reading speed by learning scale and arpeggio patterns, thereby helping one read by patterns (use metronome).

   D. Increase performance speed by mastery of scale and arpeggio patterns (use metronome).

   E. Improve on intonation in all registers (use electric tuner).

   F. Learn alternate fingerings for legato and solo style.

   G. Extend range to extreme low and high registers.

   H. Improve consistency of tone quality in all registers.

   I. Improve lip flexibility in all registers.

   J. Improve consistency of tonguing styles.

   K. Improve breath capacity and control.

   L. Improve meter and rhythm (use metronome).

   M. Improve finger, tongue, and air coordination.

   N. Improve endurance by resting between sections of the warm-up and daily routine.

II. The warm-up and daily routine.

   A. Start at the middle register and work down to the low register using a slur pattern such as in illustrations 6 (tuba range) and 7 (euphonium range). Play very slow and soft.

     1. Corners stay firm.

     2. Jaw goes in direction of pitch (never let the bottom and top teeth touch).

     3. Use mirror and metronome.

     4. Conserve your air.

     5. Work for open, relaxed throat.

6. Always rest after each selection of warm-up and daily routine.

Please note: All illustrations are applicable to both tuba and euphonium in the appropriate octave.

ILLUSTRATION NO. 6

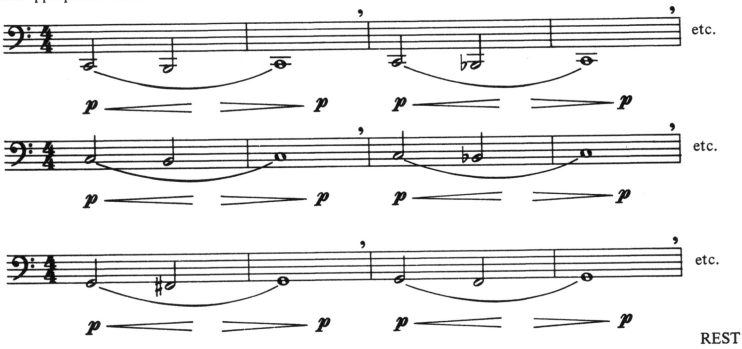

ILLUSTRATION NO. 7

B. If you are a more advanced player, play the slur pattern from the middle range down to your lower range as well as up to your high range (illustration 8).
   1. Corners firm.
   2. Play soft and at moderate speed.
   3. Continue use of mirror and metronome.
   4. Take full breaths.

ILLUSTRATION NO. 8

C. If you are an advanced player, continue your warm-up with various slur patterns to increase flexibility at a medium loud dynamic, and play through all valve combinations.

1. Check for relaxation of jaw (jaw goes in direction of pitch).
2. Check smoothness of slurs.
3. Keep corners firm (do not pull corners in high range or let corners collapse in low range—use mirror).
4. Play patterns in one breath (full breath but conserve air—use full-length mirror).

ILLUSTRATION NO. 9

REST

ILLUSTRATION NO. 10

REST

D. Increase interval slurs and expand your range to the bottom and top registers (this flexibility study will help increase endurance as well as range).
  1. Keep slurs smooth and connected (no breaks in sound or blips from valve changes).
  2. Use full tone with good control.
  3. Jaw goes in direction of pitch.
  4. Keep corners firm.
  5. When all the physical aspects of playing are working, proceed to louder dynamics.

ILLUSTRATION NO. 11

REST

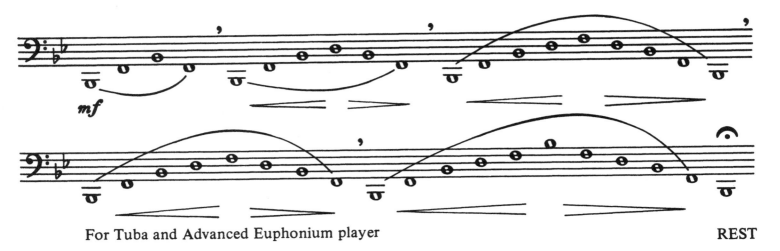

For Tuba and Advanced Euphonium player   REST

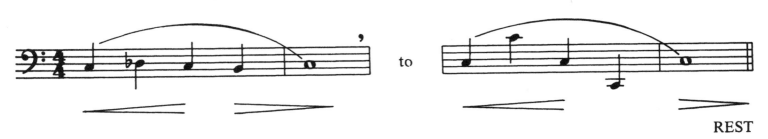

to

REST

E. The warm-up should include a legato scale and an arpeggio routine.
  1. Use metronome.
  2. Watch embouchure with mirror.
  3. Use full breaths.
  4. Play at different dynamics.
  5. Work from the middle register to your high and low registers.
  6. Scale routine should include at least one or more of the following:
     a. Major scale and arpeggio.
     b. Pure minor scale and arpeggio.
     c. Harmonic minor scale and arpeggio.
     d. Melodic minor scale and arpeggio.
     e. Chromatic scale.
     f. Whole-tone scale.
     g. Jazz diminished scale and arpeggio.
  7. Use cycle of fifths.
  8. Coordinate tongue and fingers.
  9. Rest two or three minutes before next section.

ILLUSTRATION NO. 14

REST

F. After going through your warm-up, and when all physical aspects are working correctly, proceed to or incorporate a daily routine including smears (overtone rips). See illustrations 15, 16, and 17.

   a. Middle range smears.

ILLUSTRATION NO. 15

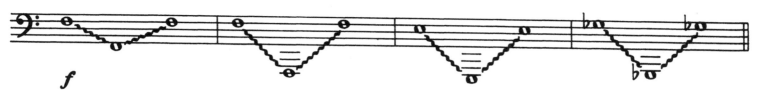

REST

   b. Middle low/high range smears.

ILLUSTRATION NO. 16

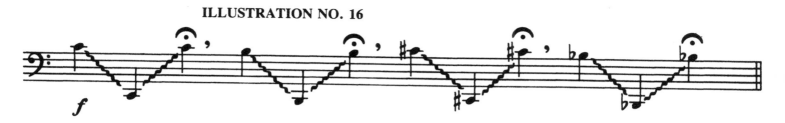

REST

   c. Extreme high/low range smears.

ILLUSTRATION NO. 17

REST

Developing and Maintaining Performing Skills

G. Tonguing routine.
  1. Single note-single tongue exercises.
  2. Vary speed with metronome.

ILLUSTRATION NO. 18

3. Double, triple tongue exercises for the advanced player.
4. Use metronome.

ILLUSTRATION NO. 19

H. Staccato scale routine.
  1. Use section E (legato scale routine).
  2. Play scales in various tempos from very slow to very fast.
  3. Use metronome.
  4. Rest for a few minutes.
I. Now you are ready for your day of practice, rehearsal(s), and/or performance(s)!
J. At the end of the day you may need or want to use part of the warm-up as a warm-down.

Chapter 5

INTONATION PROBLEMS

Discussion of intonation as related to the tuba family of instruments must consider the discrepancies between "equal temperament" (present-day tuning), "just intonation" (before major-minor system of scales), and the "harmonic overtone series" (sometimes referred to as the chord of nature). Every euphonium and tuba player should be fully familiar with intonation problems inherent to the natural harmonic overtone series. Certain partials are not the same as represented by tempered scales on the piano keyboard. Harmonic partials of the overtone series that least fit the tempered scale (counting the fundamental as 1, illustration 20) are: 5th flat, 6th sharp, 7th *extremely* flat, 11th only *approximated* pitch, 12th sharp, 13th and 14th *approximated* pitches. Illustration 20 shows the first sixteen partials of the CC tuba. The filled notes are not accurate pitches.

ILLUSTRATION NO. 20

Illustration 21 displays the B-flat euphonium harmonic overtone series (BB-flat tuba octave lower).

ILLUSTRATION NO. 21

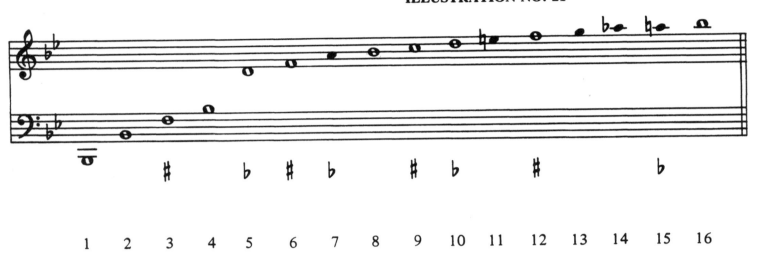

The construction of a valved brass instrument involves a series of compromises. For example, the first and second valves are generally sharp, and adjustments must be made for the noncompensating instrument. The third valve is generally built slightly flat. In addition to the problems of slide lengths, certain valve combinations have the following tendencies:

1 and 2 valve combination—slightly sharp

2 and 3 valve combination—moderately flat

1 and 3 valve combination—very sharp

1, 2, 3 valve combination—extremely sharp

Each addition of a valve theoretically makes each note approximately 6 percent more sharp as seen in table 5.1. These intonation problems may be tempered by various types of compensating systems or by manually lengthening the first and/or third valve slides. The "automatic" compensating system is convenient but may not be as accurate overall as adjusting (pulling) slides or as a properly tuned fifth valve. Individual players should innovate their own approach or system of adjusting the valve slides of a particular instrument for accommodating preferred valve combinations and pitch adjustments.

Table 5.1

Valves Used	*Semitone change due to Valves Used*	*Percent Increase in Effective Length*
0	0	0
2	1	5.95%
1	2	12.25%
1,2	3	18.92%
2,3	4	25.99%
1,3	5	33.48%
1,2,3	6	41.42%

The inherent intonation problems of the three-valved baritone or euphonium are similar to those of the cornet and other three-valve instruments. However, an entirely new set of intonation possibilities occurs with the introduction of a fourth valve. The pitch of the fourth valve usually approximates a perfect fourth lower than the fundamental (alternate to the 1-3 combination and similar to the F attachment on the trombone).

The automatic compensating system is meant to solve problems of low-register intonation, especially the 1-3 and 1-2-3 valve combinations. In 1874 this system was incorporated by David Blaikley for baritones, euphoniums, and tubas built in England. There are three and four valve automatic compensating systems. In this system each valve contains a second loop of tubing which is to correct intonation when used in combination with a master valve. In the four valve system corrective lengths of tubing are automatically added when the fourth valve is used in combination with other valves. The first three valves perform normally when used independently of the fourth valve. While the three and four valve automatic compensating systems do improve intonation to some degree, they are not a final solution to intonation problems, thus alternate fingerings continue to be an important consideration. The four valve system is essential for players beyond the beginning level. As with the non-compensating system, good intonation really depends on players getting to know the idiosyncracies of each of their individual instruments. At this writing, the automatic compensating system is only available on top-action instruments.

Players are cautioned not to depend solely on the four-valve instrument as a fully satisfactory solution to intonation problems, though, admittedly, many out-of-tune pitches can be adjusted by use of the fourth valve or combinations using the fourth valve. Adjustment of pitches can also be made by manipulating a particular valve slide, if the slide is conveniently placed. As with any brass instrument, the well-trained ear of the performer coupled with automatic lip adjustments is the best assurance of good intonation. Low register fingerings on the euphonium are commensurate with the fingerings used on a BB-flat tuba, only an octave higher. In illustration 22, the recommended fingering for the compensating euphonium is notated above the staff. Any difference with the noncompensating euphonium is noted below the staff.

Please note that the low C-flat (1-2-3) produced on the noncompensating B-flat euphonium and tuba is an "induced" or false tone. Also note that for the purposes of better intonation, the fourth valve is very often used in preference to the 1-3 valve combination, especially in European (mostly German) instruments. For the same reason, the 2-4 valve combination is most always preferred to the 1-2-3 valve combination.

Basic intonation and tonal quality of the euphonium and tuba is also influenced by proper breath support, embouchure control, and sensitive, intelligent listening. All members of the tuba family have common considerations relative to tone production, intonation, and

Please note: 1. Fingerings in parentheses are induced or fake tones.

2. Finger combinations with the 4th valve normally improve intonation.

technique. However, each instrument within the family has particular peculiarities with which the student, teacher, and artist/performer must cope. Also, playing characteristics of available instruments will differ as each manufacturer endeavors to innovate and compete on the open market. Therefore, it is virtually impossible to document or illustrate all the varying personal attitudes and concepts of today's performers, and to attempt so would be more confusing than helpful. The intention, then, is to concentrate on pedagogical and the most common mechanical considerations to offer some clarification for better understanding and artistic musical application.

The acoustical phenomenon of induced tones is explained by Dr. Arthur Benade of Case Western Reserve University as follows: "These 'privileged' or 'false' tones are produced by buzzing the lips on the mouthpiece as any other note (the second partial 'B♭', the third partial 'F' help produce this particular range on the BB♭ tuba and euphonium). A player can hear and feel the vibrations of sound; since the air column is moving very slowly, one can give a push on the second swing of the sound wave."[1] It is a gap that can be played, but not with the same quality of regular tone.

An essential step to checking overall intonation of a particular euphonium or tuba is to first determine the intonation of the open tones; then second valve; first valve; third valve; combinations 1-2; 2-3; 1-4; fourth valve; 1-2-3; 2-4; 1-2; 1-2-4; 3-4; 2-3-4; 1-3-4; 1-2-3-4. If the instrument has a fifth or sixth valve, then similar testing of possible combinations should be done. Ideally, checking on an instrument's intonation should be done with a "strobe" and results documented on manuscript paper. Such testing should be done periodically. It is important that a player know the intonation characteristics of his instrument(s) thoroughly (see illustration 23).

ILLUSTRATION NO. 23

Euphonium

BB♭ Tuba

CC Tuba

E♭ Tuba

F Tuba

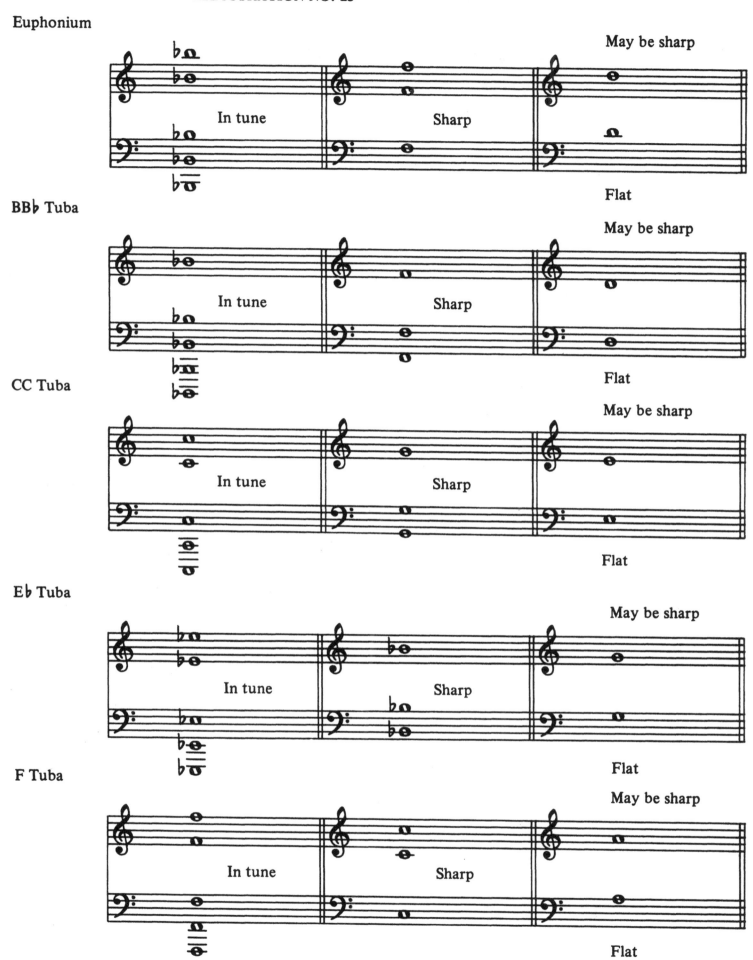

However, instrument companies may alter the notes somewhat, as shown in illustration 24.

The previous examples represent the general approach commonly adhered to by most manufacturers. Some manufacturers raise the sixth partial to bring the fifth partial in tune, while others keep the sixth partial in tune, retaining the fifth as partially flat.

Valve intonation tendencies are quite similar to the other brass instruments, but the degree of pitch problems seems to increase proportionately with the size of the instrument. A tuba with relatively "in tune" open tones should have easily and comfortably accessible first, third, and fourth valve slides that can be manipulated with the left hand. An instrument with an accessible main tuning slide, either directly operated by the left hand or via a rod extension, is also a good feature for determining whether to pull or push the upper-valve slide of the noncompensating euphonium-baritone, BB-flat tuba, CC tuba, E-flat tuba, and F tuba.

ILLUSTRATION NO. 24

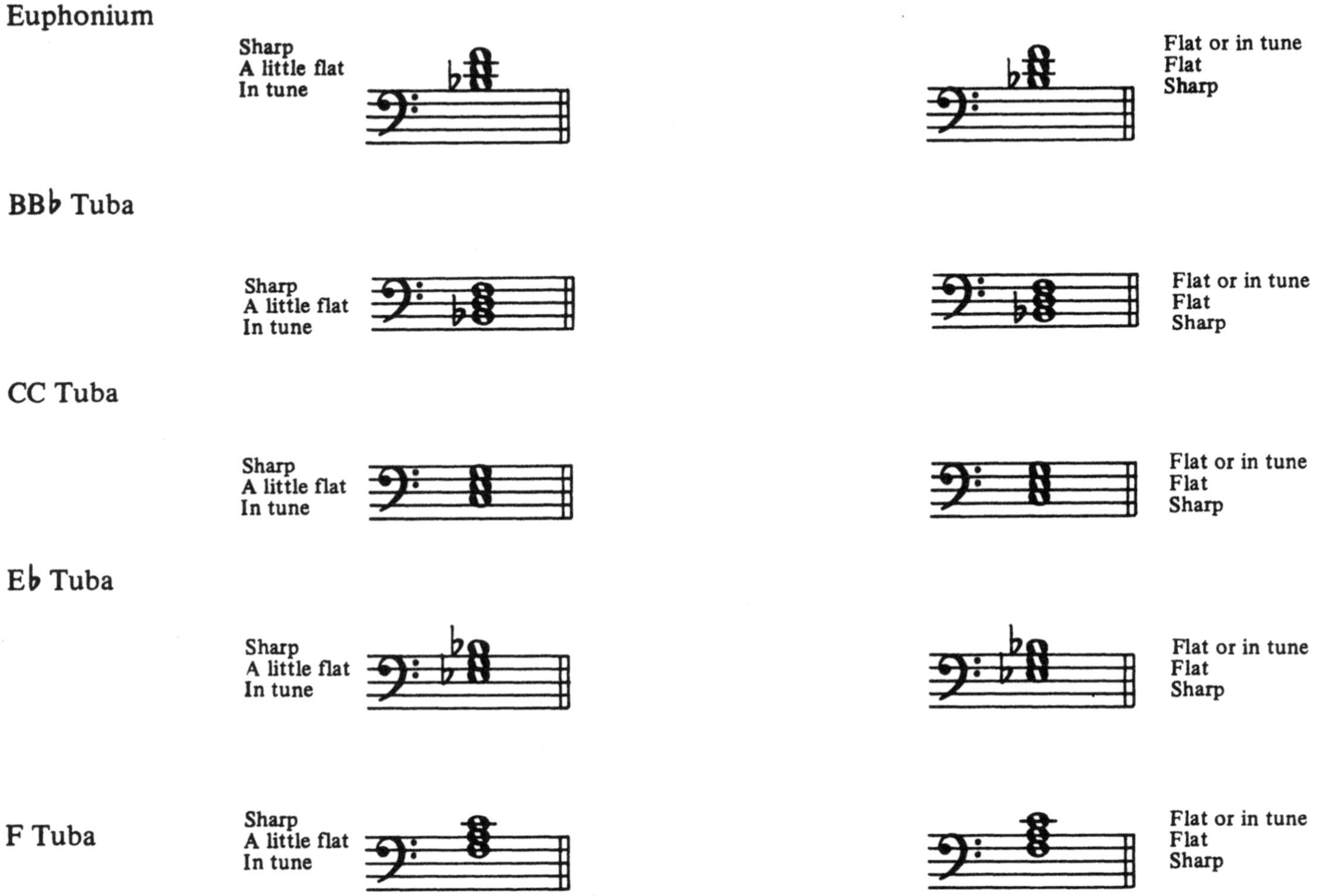

Euphonium-Baritone

↑ Pull (lengthen) valve slide or lip down
↓ Push (shorten) valve slide or lip up

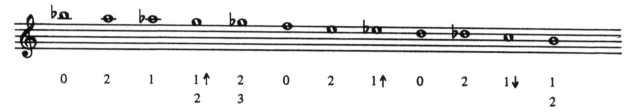

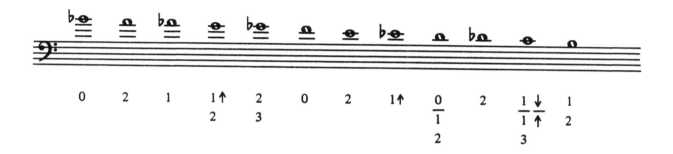

Many manufacturers provide the fifth valve as a flat whole step (1¼ steps); however, some design the fifth valve as a two whole step (2/3 system). Either system is effective depending on personal preference.

ILLUSTRATION NO. 26

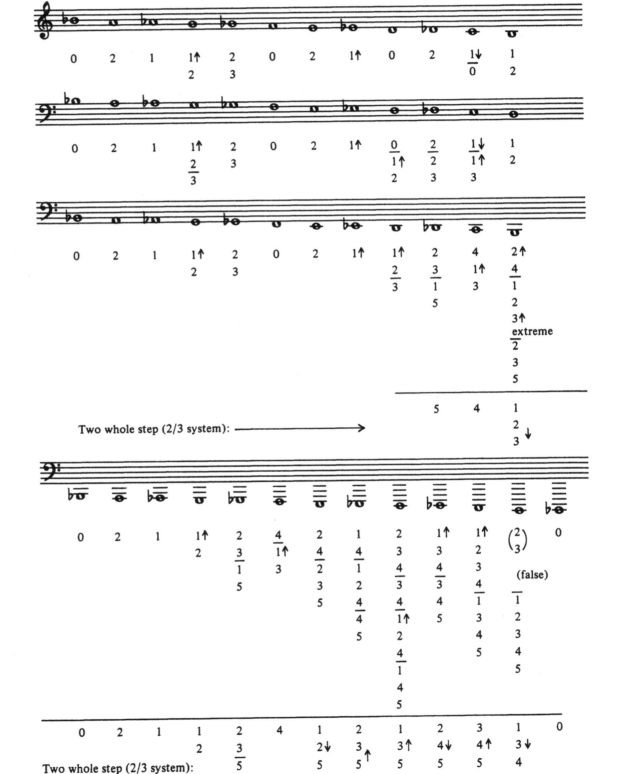

BB♭ Tuba
↑ Pull (lengthen) valve slide or lip down
↓ Push (shorten) valve slide or lip up

THE ART OF TUBA AND EUPHONIUM

Many manufacturers provide the fifth valve as a flat whole step (1¼ steps); however, some design the fifth valve as a two whole step (2/3 system). Either system is effective depending on personal preference.

ILLUSTRATION NO. 27

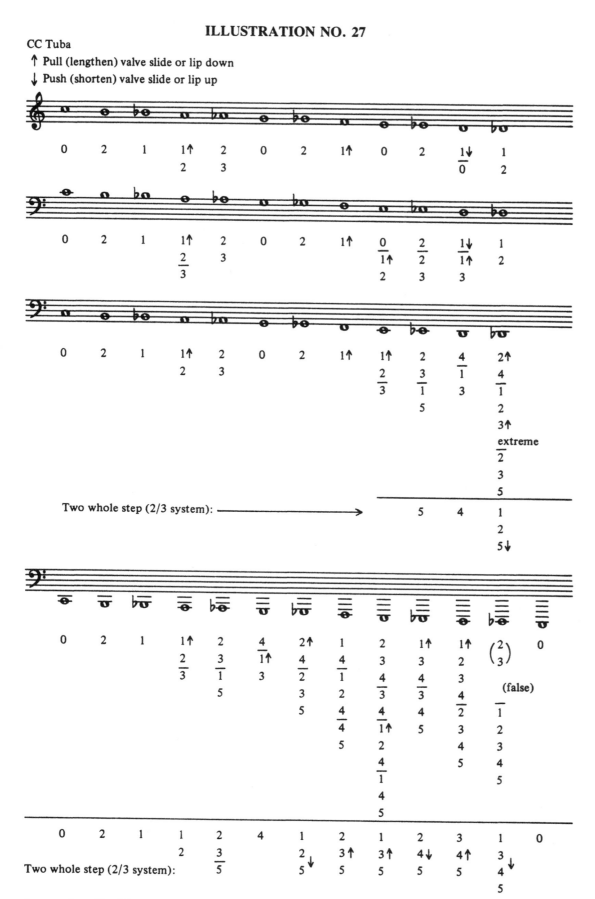

CC Tuba

↑ Pull (lengthen) valve slide or lip down
↓ Push (shorten) valve slide or lip up

Intonation Problems

Eb Tuba
↑ Pull (lengthen) valve slide or lip down
↓ Push (shorten) valve slide or lip down
*5th valve flat whole step

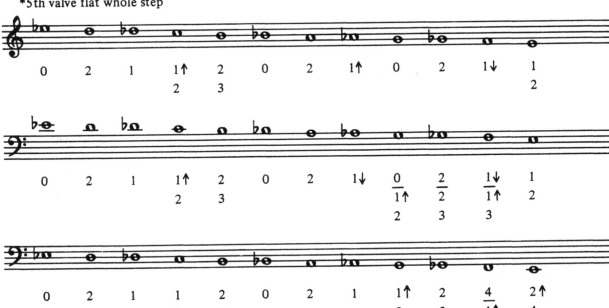

ILLUSTRATION NO. 29

F Tuba

↑ Pull (lengthen) valve slide or lip down

↓ Push (shorten) valve slide or lip up

*5th valve flat whole step

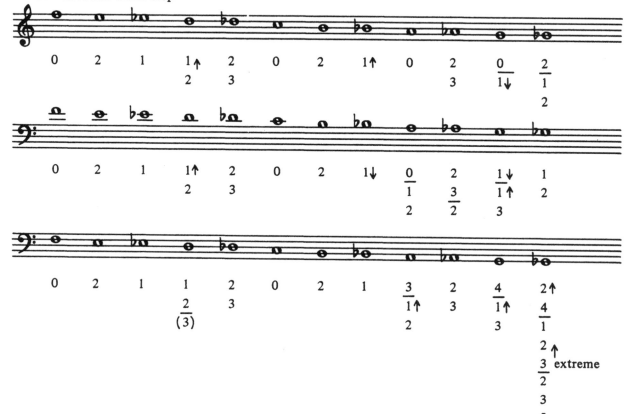

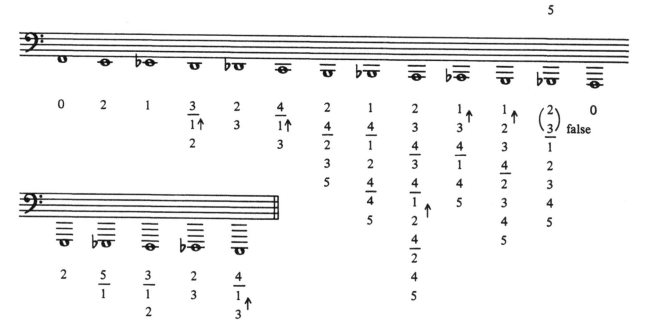

Intonation Problems

As indicated by illustrations in this chapter, four general conclusions should be observed:

1. With the exception of the open upper fundamental and open fifth partial (both likely to be quite sharp), the very top range of the euphonium and tuba is likely to be disturbingly flat. This requires the player to listen carefully and to correct intonation with the lip (first preference) or by either adjusting valve tubing lengths (second preference) or using alternate valve combinations (third preference).

2. The very bottom range of the euphonium and tuba is quite likely to be disturbingly sharp. Intonation of some notes may be corrected with the lip, but severe discrepancies will need to be adjusted by lengthening valve tubing (pulling slides) or with alternate valve combination.

3. Utilizing the proper "method book" valve combinations given for euphonium and tuba (even in the mid-range) is never a guarantee that correct intonation will result.

4. The combination of well-trained and sensitive ears with a strong and flexible embouchure is really a player's "main tuning slide," with adjusted length of valve tubing and alternate valve combinations as second and third alternatives for adjusting intonation.

In illustration 30 the three low notes are most always acoustically sharp, while the upper note is flat. Many instrument manufacturers correct this latter discrepancy by shortening the first valve tubing. The sharpness of the three lower notes must then be corrected by pulling (neutralizing) the first valve slide with the left hand. Also, if there is a fourth valve, the fingerings in parentheses can usually be used to correct intonation. On some instruments it may be desirable to use the third valve instead of the 1-2 combination and fourth valve instead of the 1-3 combination.

The first valve slide is most often used for pitch adjustment, although adjusting the length of other valve slides can also be calibrated to alter the pitch of notes associated with them. Some players prefer using the main tuning slide almost exclusively for pitch adjustment, especially on tubas with vertical moving main tuning slides.

In addition to basic three-valve instruments, many tubas have four, five, six, or even seven valves. It is common to have the fourth valve pitched a perfect fourth below the fundamental (alternate to 1-3 combination), and, while the fifth valve is generally a major third below the keynote, some players prefer to have it a second below. The length of tubing and basic pitch for each additional valve is both personal and controversial.

The fingering for the four-valve tuba is directly related to that of the euphonium. In illustration 31, a fingering chart for a three- and four-valve BB-flat tuba and euphonium are given for the low register. The three-valve euphonium and tuba fingerings are given above the illustration. Preferred four-valve fingering combinations are given below the illustration. Please note differences between compensating and noncompensating instruments. Fingerings in parentheses are induced or false tones.

ILLUSTRATION NO. 30

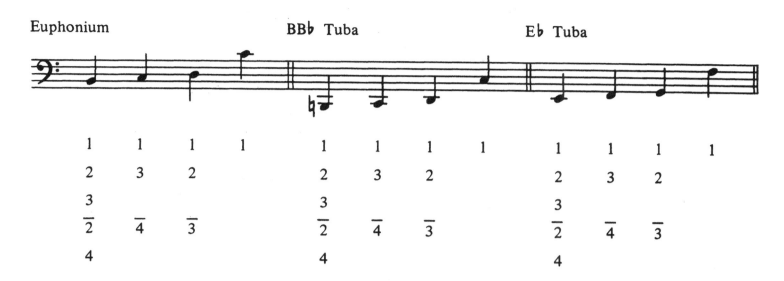

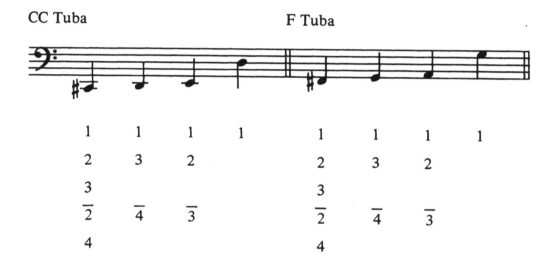

Three-Valve

Compensating:

1	1	0	2	1	1	2	1	1	(0)	(2)	(1)	(1 2)	(2 3)	0
3	2				2	3	3	2						
	3							3						

Non-compensating:

1	1	0	2	1	1	2	1	1	(0)	(2)	(1)	(1 2)	(2 3)	
3	2				2	3	3	2						0
	3							3						

Euphonium:

BBb Tuba:

Four-Valve

Compensating:

4	2	0	2	1	1	2	4	2	1	1	2	1	1	0
	4				2	3		4	4	2	3	3	2	
										4	4	4	3	
													4	

Non-compensating:

4	2	0	2	1	1	2	4	2	1	2	1	1	(2 3)	0
	4				2	3		4	4	3	3	2		
										4	4	3		
												4		

On the three-valve BB-flat tuba and euphonium, E-flat to low B natural are induced or false tones. The low B natural on the noncompensating four-valve tuba and euphonium is also an induced or false note. On a five-valve BB tuba (fifth valve, a major third below keynote), the low B natural would be played 1-2-3-4-5, while the low B-flat could be played with the valve combination or open.

Illustration 32 offers some suggested tuning solutions for the BB-flat tuba (these suggestions are also applicable to tubas in CC, E-flat, F, and euphonium with transposed adjustment for each particular instrument).

Other factors that influence intonation on the tuba are:

1. A flabby relaxation of the embouchure in the low register; this causes you to play slightly flat.

2. Tightness of the embouchure in the lower register; this causes you to play sharp.

3. Top register has a tendency to be sharp.

4. Variation in pitch due to temperature—hot (sharp) or cold (flat).

Proper breath support and correct embouchure that responds to a well-trained ear can usually adjust most of the inherent intonation problems of the euphonium and tuba.

ILLUSTRATION NO. 32

These open notes might be sharp. You need to lip down or adjust by extending the main tuning slide by pulling out. (An alternate fingering would be 1-3.)

The top note will probably be flat. You need to lip up or adjust the main tuning slide by pushing in. (Alternative fingering for 1-2 is 3.) If you use 1-2, you will probably need to pull the first slide.

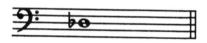

This note is usually flat on the second valve. You need to lip up. This note may also be fingered 2-3. The third valve slide may need to be pulled.

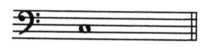

This note will probably be flat. You need to push the first valve slide in. This note also might need to be lipped up in addition to using the slide. (Alternate fingering is 1-3.)

Footnotes
1. Arthur Benade, interview with William Winkle, February 19, 1980.

Chapter 6

SELECTION OF A MOUTHPIECE

Students (and some teachers) place too much emphasis on the selection of a mouthpiece for beginning students. Most instrument makers are conscientious about providing a mouthpiece with each model of instrument, and they recommend the mouthpiece as being suited to good results on that particular instrument. As a student progresses, improves, gains a concept of sound and flexibility, and strengthens his embouchure, he may—but only with the guidance and recommendations of his teacher—wish to test and select another mouthpiece, hopefully of ideal suitability. It is only after years of practice that most players feel the need for a change of mouthpiece. Some points to consider in evaluating choices of mouthpieces are:

1. Be sure the mouthpiece is plated and not scarred or dented.

2. Beware of "trick" or "special" mouthpieces, especially those of wide rims and so-called (extreme) cushion mouthpieces. The rim of the mouthpiece is a primary factor in developing flexibility and in controlling the focus of sound. For example, a sharp rim may help focus the sound more evenly, but at the sacrifice of flexibility.

3. The mouthpiece cup should be of medium depth to best accommodate the mid-range and also allow both the high and low range to "speak" properly.

4. The back bore of the mouthpiece should fit the bore of the instrument.

5. People with strong (or large) embouchures generally get better results with larger and deeper mouthpieces. Those with weaker (or smaller) embouchures will usually find a smaller and shallower mouthpiece more suitable.

6. A mouthpiece should fit the bore of an instrument. More often than not, such a mouthpiece will come with the instrument.

7. It is strongly recommended that a player's primary mouthpiece allow maximum results of tone quality, flexibility, and tech-

nique in the middle register (two octaves) and also permit full access to the extreme ranges.

The brass mouthpiece is really nothing more than a pre-amplifying piece of equipment. It is designed to pick up the sound waves of a vibrating source—the lips—then organize and project these vibrations into (or through) a specified length of tubing. This process should result in a specific musical pitch. A cupped mouthpiece is an enlargement of the bore (of the instrument), to which the player's lips are applied, forming a kind of double reed. Very little is written on the history of the mouthpiece, but it is probably safe to assume that in its earliest stage it was nothing more than a hole in a ram's horn (as with the shofar) or a conch shell into which the player projected air and buzzed his lips. Formerly, some mouthpieces were wrought from sheet metal hammered to shape and joined down the side. Ivory, horn, and hard woods have also been used to make mouthpieces.

A general listing of the characteristics of various cup mouthpieces follows in the next section. These characteristics of mouthpieces very considerably. The euphonium mouthpiece varies from a deep cup to an almost conical shape. The tuba mouthpiece is more or less conical but is generally cupped to some extent.

There are six basic component parts of a mouthpiece:
1. bite (or inner rim)
2. rim
3. cup
4. throat
5. backbore
6. shank

These are shown in illustration 33, and the following paragraphs will discuss the general ways in which each of these component parts affects the tone.

ILLUSTRATION NO. 33

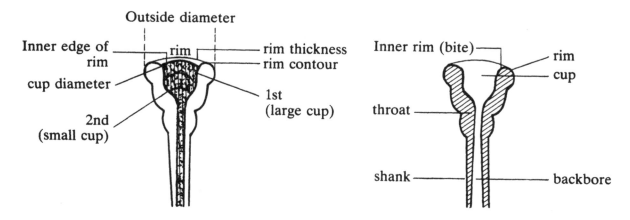

The bite: The relative sharpness or roundness of the bite (inner rim) affects articulation. Generally, the sharper the bite, the sharper the articulation. Likewise, the more rounded the inner rim, the easier it becomes to slur. When selecting a cup mouthpiece it is important to balance these two variants (rounded bite; sharp bite) to achieve optimum flexibility while retaining a clear, concise articulation. The inner rim will also affect the ease with which the upper and/or lower range is produced. Generally speaking, the wider the inner rim, the easier the low notes respond, and the narrower the rim, the easier the high notes respond.

The rim: The choice of an outer rim, (width and contour, flat or rounded) is largely a matter of comfort. The inner rim or bite may be sharp or rounded. An excessively wide rim will reduce flexibility and affect tone quality. The basic determining factor relating to the width of the rim (besides comfort) should be the relative strength or weakness of your embouchure. A stronger embouchure can usually manage a wider rim.

The cup: The depth and diameter (volume) of the mouthpiece cup is perhaps the most important single factor affecting overall efficiency. Generally, as a brass player develops, he will consider moving to a larger-size cup. This concept is based on the premise that the diameter of the larger cup allows more lip to vibrate, producing a fuller sound, richer in harmonics.

As the large cup provides a fuller sound, it also facilitates the production of the lower register. Conversely, a smaller, shallower cup tends to produce a brighter (possibly more focused) sound and allows for easier production of the higher register.

The throat and backbore: The shape and diameter of the mouthpiece throat and backbore further affects the tone quality of a brass instrument. Simply stated, the larger the backbore, the bigger and darker the tone. However, if the bore is too large, the tone may not be centered and become diffused. The backbore affects a player's ability to produce the higher register. If the backbore is basically cylindrical and has very little flare, it can aid in the production of the higher register but cause the low register to be more difficult to produce. It may also hinder the production of a big sound. If the backbore is basically conical, the tone will tend to open up, and a good deal of volume can be produced; however, the production of the upper register may be hindered. It appears that if the backbore is cylindrical for a short distance and then conical to the end, the tone is much easier to control. The throat of the mouthpiece helps facilitate control of intonation and response. Teachers often encourage students to use larger-sized mouthpieces as they develop stronger embouchures. Careful guidance and moderation is called for in this regard.

Conclusion

In selecting a preferred mouthpiece for each player, one must consider the teeth, jaw, and size and shape (thickness and width) of the lips as well as the developed strength of his embouchure. Desired tone quality, ease of playing the complete register, intonation, endurance, and the type of playing done most of the time are also important factors to consider.

As stated before, the larger cup diameter of a mouthpiece allows for more lip vibration, which should produce a tone richer in harmonics. A small cup depth used with a large rim will aid the clarity of tone, especially with a large tuba.

The rim helps determine the flexibility of the tone. A checklist for special needs is as follows:

High register—Decrease the cup diameter and the depth of the cup. Use smaller bore mouthpiece.

Low register—Increase the cup diameter and depth. Use a larger bore mouthpiece.

Darker tone—Use a deeper cup mouthpiece.

Brighter tone—Use a shallower, bowl-shaped cup.

Staccato—Use a sharper inner rim (bite).

Accurate attacks—Use a sharper inner rim (bite).

More flexibility—Use a rounder inner rim (bite).

Slurs—Use a rounder rim (bite).

Less resistance—Use a larger throat.

More resistance—Use a smaller throat.

Strong endurance—Use a small to large cup with narrow to wide rim.

Weak endurance—Use a medium wide rim with small to medium cup.

Beware of changing mouthpieces every time there is a problem in one or more of the above traits. A primary mouthpiece should be selected to suit you and to best accommodate the specific type of playing you do the majority of the time. Different types of mouthpieces become a personal choice for concert band (military band), symphony orchestra, chamber ensemble, solo performance, recording studio (radio/television work), dance work, jazz, or rock.

In selecting a mouthpiece for the tuba, baritone, or euphonium, make sure the shank of the mouthpiece fits snugly into the instrument. If it does not fit snugly there may be need for a shank adaptor or for having the shank taper adjusted by a good mouthpiece maker or instrument repairman. Screw-on inner changeable rims are popular types of mouthpieces commonly used by advanced students and professional players. New (sometimes innovative) baritone, euphonium, and tuba mouthpieces are constantly being developed as players continue to seek perfection (or a bit of magic!).

Contrary to some teachers' opinions, the tubist is as sensitive to differences in mouthpiece models and styles as are his brass instrument colleagues. As with any other brass instrument, the type and style of music being performed, coupled with a specific instrument model and player preference, will dictate the size and model of mouthpiece selected.

The most famous and most copied tuba mouthpiece was designed by August Helleberg (1857–1931) and first produced by the C. G. Conn Company. Today Conn offers the Conn Helleberg 7B 1070 (small) and Conn Helleberg 1090 (large). Other mouthpiece makers also produce their own Helleberg mouthpiece; there is considerable variation from one to another.

As previously mentioned, the mouthpiece provided by the manufacturer for a particular instrument model should be given consideration. Another mouthpiece may be contemplated if there are problems, but (again) students are cautioned to select only with guidance from their teacher. If one is to spend several hundred or several thousand dollars for a particular instrument, he should have respect for the manufacturer of that instrument and seriously consider the mouthpiece provided and/or recommended for it.

Chapter 7

TAKING CARE OF YOUR INSTRUMENT

It is wise to follow the manufacturer's instructions for "breaking in" a new instrument. In most cases the exclusive use of quality valve oil is recommended; others recommend oil and water. In any case it is important to keep the valves, valve casing, slides, and the entire instrument clean—inside and out.

It is extremely important to keep the mouthpiece clean. Do this by removing all particles of dirt with a mouthpiece brush and clean, running water. Avoid leaving the mouthpiece in the instrument after playing. In case of a stuck mouthpiece, *never* use pliers or force in any way, but use a mouthpiece puller (available at your local repair shop or in your teacher's studio). Mouthpiece shank dents and bit or extension dents should always be removed by a qualified repairman.

The inside tubing of brass instruments should be cleaned regularly by flushing warm water through it. Never use hot water to clean any brass instrument. A "snake" brush (length of coil with brush on each end) is most helpful. Be careful not to dent the tubing. Dents will weaken the walls of the tubing, affect the tuning of the instrument, and look bad. Also, the removal of dents will further weaken walls of the tubing. A qualified instrument maker or repairman should remove all dents.

When cleaning a piston valve instrument, work the valves up and down while a stream of warm water is flushed through the instrument. When the instrument is thoroughly clean, water emitted from the tubing should run clear. Dirty valves and valve casings are the most common cause of sluggish valve action. Valves may be cleaned with mild soap and water, but all soap film must be rinsed away.

Do not use soaps containing abrasives: They are likely to scratch and damage the valves. If soap is to be used, use only castile soap such as Ivory. For the valve casings, use a cleaning rod and clean cheesecloth (or linen). Be extremely careful that the metal rod does not touch the casing wall and that fragments of the cheesecloth do not catch onto sharp edges. Rinse valves and valve casings with clean, warm water before replacing the valves and/or applying oil to them.

Keep tuning slides and valve slides clean. Ordinarily, soap and water will do, but if the slides have become corroded, it may be necessary to use a mild metal polish to restore the finish. Be careful not to polish away too much of the metal surface. Before replacing the slides, wipe them clean, flush with clean water, and lubricate with a small amount of slide grease.

For instruments with lacquer finish, the outside tubing can be cleaned with clean water and a chamois, or for better results a good quality lacquer cleaner may be used. Never use silver polish, commercial cleaning fluids, or any cleaner that contains alcohol on lacquered instruments.

Silver-plated instruments may be cleaned with a clear tarnish remover (such as Tarn-X) but must be rinsed thoroughly and immediately (follow directions). Almost any high-quality silver polish can be used as long as it is not gritty and abrasive. All silver polishes will remove some plating and should therefore be used in moderation—*keep your instrument clean.* Silver polish paste can be made of "whiting powder" and alcohol; plain whiting powder on a cloth will work also. However, since some silver-plated instruments are lacquered, precaution must be taken with any use of an alcohol cleaner/polish. Cloths containing jewelers rouge can be obtained at jewelry stores. These "jewelers cloths" will help to keep silver instruments clean and attractive.

Good care and maintenance should be a priority for every instrumentalist (student or professional). Preventive maintenance helps to keep the instrument out of the repair shop. Observe the following:

Care of the Instrument

I. Clean and sterilize mouthpiece on a regular basis at least once a week (rinse the mouth before playing, or better yet, brush teeth and rinse).

II. Sterilize bits (extensions) once a week. If they are lacquered do not use hot water or any substance that will damage or remove the lacquer.

III. In preparing to clean your whole instrument, the following sequence should be followed:

A. Oiling and cleaning your valves.

1. Piston valve instruments. Unscrew top valve caps and take out the valves as you remove them from the casing. Keep them in order and set aside in a container of water. Do not drop. Using a clean cloth, wipe all oil off the valves, and put them back in the container of water. Next, remove the springs and valve caps. Wipe old grease off the spring, and keep them in order by tagging (or numbering) them according to their corresponding valve. Also, clean the top and bottom valve caps and set them aside in order.

2. Rotary valve instruments. Unscrew bottom valve cap and wide excess oil or grease before oiling the bushing under

the valve cap. Also oil the bushing under the stop arm and lever. Be sure to oil all moveable parts of the rotary valve, including the spring. Clean the valve caps. If the rotary valves are quite tight, the valve oil will have to be put into valve tubing for each valve to keep the valves free as well as improve the action and speed of the valves. A student should dismantle a rotary valve only with the careful guidance of a teacher (dismantling a rotary valve will be discussed later in this chapter).

B. Pull all slides and wipe off the old grease. Flush and brush clean the inside tubing of each slide. Set them safely aside in order.

C. Using liquid detergent in warm water, flush the entire horn or submerge the body of the instrument in warm water and allow it to soak for ten to fifteen minutes (or longer). The family bathtub works very nicely (especially with spray attachment) for a tuba or euphonium. Repeat this process until all foreign matter is removed from the inside of the slide tubing. Flush and run a snake brush through the leadpipe and instrument body. Rinse well.

D. Once the valves and the body of the horn have been cleaned, wipe the entire horn dry and reassemble it carefully and in an orderly fashion (careful of piston valve springs and valves).

E. It is also a good idea to smear a little slide grease or oil on the threads of the top and bottom valve caps (be careful not to get grease on the valve or valve casing).

   1. Piston valves: Use quality oil generously and regularly. When needed, replace worn felt and cork bumpers for correct alignment and quieter action. Better-made piston valve instruments will have minimum tolerance between valve and casing and are more apt to become sluggish when dry or dirty. Saliva acids will cause corrosion. When doing outdoor parades or concerts, it is important to keep the valves well oiled (be certain to clean the instrument immediately after such an outside performance).

   2. Rotary valves: Valves should be oiled regularly. Rotary valves can be oiled without disassembling the entire valve as mentioned in the care of the instrument outline. Place a few drops of oil on each bushing, and lubricate the rotor by placing a few drops of oil in each crook (valve slide), allowing the oil to run into the valve. Oil should also be placed in the thread of the caps of the rotary valve. Oiling only the stem (bushing) alone is not adequate; all movable parts of the rotary valve mechanism must be lubricated. This will help the mechanism to operate quieter and faster. Better rotary valve instruments will have minimum tolerance between valve and casing and are more apt to become sluggish when dry or dirty. Rotary valves should normally be left in the casings. However, if there are special problems with rotary valves, only a qualified repairman or an experienced teacher should remove them.

Dismantling a Rotary Valve

I. Tools needed for dismantling a rotary valve.
   A. Small rawhide hammer or wooden hammer.
   B. Slot screwdriver.
   C. Wooden dowel (approximately $6'' \times \frac{1}{2}''$ diameter—a cut off drumstick works well). A 2″ to 3″ aluminum rod ($\frac{1}{6}''$ to $\frac{3}{16}''$ diameter) could be used (piccolo tuning/cleaning rod with a cut off end works also).
   D. Various weights of valve oil.
   E. Cleaning cloth, Q-Tips, or other suitable cleaning aids.
II. Dismantling a rotary valve.
   A. The tools should be placed across your lap or on a flat table with a towel on it.
   B. Remove screw from top of valve stem that holds on stop arm (see illustrations 34, 35, and 36). Slowly and gently pry the stop arm off the valve stem (tapered fit) by levering against the cork plate (credit card) on top of casing.
   C. Remove bottom valve cap (dust cap).
   D. Tap gently with a rawhide hammer on the raised stop screw. This will drive the rotary out of the casing, and, in turn, the back bearing will drop out (place free hand below the valve to catch the back bearing).
   E. With your horn across your lap or on a table, place your hand behind the valve, ready to catch it. Tap straight down on stem with the mallet (the mallet must be softer than brass, for instance, a rawhide mallet; *never* use a metal hammer) until back-plate is free and the rotor falls into your hand. If the stop arm does not come off easily in step B, you will use the aluminum rod (much softer than brass) to tap rotor and back-plate out of the casing and stop arm all at once. Enlist someone to help as "catcher" (or place a pillow behind the valve so it won't fall to the floor or table). Make sure the aluminum rod is small enough to pass into the opening of the stop arm. You may have to sand or file a "flat" on the rod to fit the shape of the hole. Warnings: Always use materials softer than the brass (wood or rawhide mallet, wood or aluminum rod). Tap straight down on stem or rod. Side blows may bend the valve stem. Some back-plates are stubborn to pound out, but you won't damage the plate or rotor if you follow these rules. When in doubt, contact a qualified repair person.
III. Cleaning and oiling rotary valve.
   A. Clean the rotor and the back-plate with warm soapy water, being careful not to bang parts around. You may soak them for a short time in white vinegar if they are coated with mineral oil. (If they do not clean up, have your horn chemically cleaned by an experienced repairman.)
   B. Put a small amount of a slightly heavier oil on the shafts of the rotor (3 in 1 or even regular motor oil). A light valve oil should be reserved for "outside body" surfaces of the rotor.

ILLUSTRATION 34

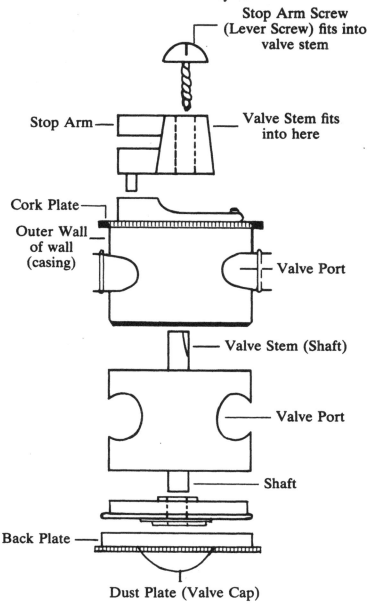

Dismantled Rotary Valve

Stop Arm Screw
(Lever Screw) fits into
valve stem

Stop Arm —

Valve Stem fits
into here

Cork Plate —

Outer Wall
of wall
(casing)

Valve Port

Valve Stem (Shaft)

Valve Port

Shaft

Back Plate —

Dust Plate (Valve Cap)

IV. Installation of rotary valves.
   A. Place the horn backside up on your lap or on a table.
   B. After oiling shafts, drop the rotor back down into casing, then reach around and push it back up slightly so you can oil the circumference of the rotor body with light valve oil. Twirl the rotor as you drop oil at the edge. Then let the rotor fall back into the casing.
   C. Take a large wooden dowel and a mallet and tap the back plate down into the casing by moving the dowel around the outer edge in a circular motion, tapping lightly with the mallet. You should be able to hear the sound of the taps change when the plate is completely back in.

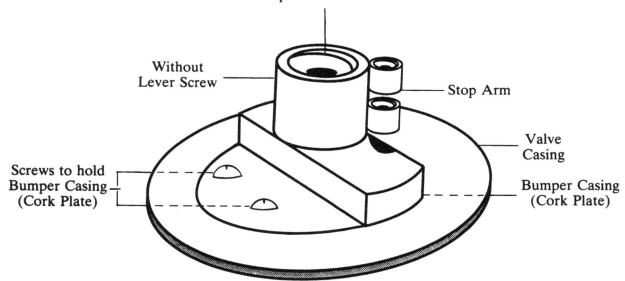

Top of Rotary Valve

NOTICE: Flat shaped fourth side of valve stem

D. Check the rotor to see if it turns freely. If it is locked up, either the back-plate is not fully seated in the casing (continue to tap it in) or, as is the case with many valves, the back-plate when fully in place binds the rotor. To correct this, simply tap the top stem lightly to level the back-plate, and the rotor should turn freely.

E. If the rotor turns freely, place the stop arm back onto the rotor stem and replace the screw. Replace the back dust cap (valve cap).

Warnings: If the rotor does not work, remove it and check for dirt or other foreign matter on the rotor or in the casing. If it still does not want to work, the casing or the rotor may still have too much scale and dirt buildup, or the valve may have been nicked or bent. In any case, take the horn to a qualified repair person. Never sand, file, or attempt to straighten a rotor. Clearances are very precise (.001″), and a lot of damage can be done if you don't know how to repair the problem!

Many services are available at music stores with excellent instrument repair shops, including the following: (1) cleaning valves and/or horn by acid dip treatment; (2) replating mouthpieces; (3) relacquering/replating instrument; and (4) overhauling instrument and taking out small dents. Any of these services, including a major overhaul of an instrument, should be considered carefully and made in consultation with a qualified repairman.

A checklist for instrument care follows.

Oil valves regularly (residue on valves cause wear and result in their deterioration).

Grease their valve (residue on slides cause wear and result in deterioration of an instrument). *Do not use vaseline.*

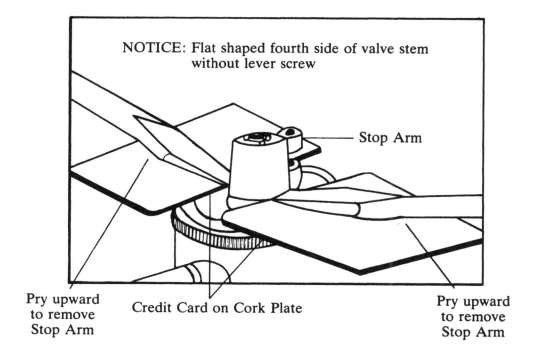

NOTICE: Flat shaped fourth side of valve stem without lever screw

— Stop Arm

Pry upward to remove Stop Arm

Credit Card on Cork Plate

Pry upward to remove Stop Arm

The springs of the valve (piston or rotary) should be given a thin coat of grease.

Some tuba and euphonium manufacturers suggest dropping a little oil in the leadpipe to break in a new instrument.

Wipe oil onto the shank of the mouthpiece and onto the bits to prevent sticking. This practice will help prevent corrosion from saliva acids.

Occasionally check if pranksters have used your instrument as a repository for such items as a music folio, band uniform plumes, or wastepaper or any other discarded items.

Check the water key cork(s) for wear and leaks; be certain they are air tight.

Maintain a service kit and keep it with your instrument. Items and materials that should be included in a service kit are as follows:

A. Flexible valve brush and mouthpiece brush
B. Medium bristle toothbrush
C. Valve cleaning rod (22 cal. rifle rod)
D. Snake brush
E. Valve oil (light and heavy for rotary valve)
F. Slide grease
G. Several clean rags (cheesecloth as well as linen type of material)
H. Chamois cloth
I. Castile soap
J. Screwdrivers for key and rotary valve mechanism
K. Rawhide, wood, or hard rubber hammer (for removing rotary valves)

Taking Care of Your Instrument

L. Extra pads, corks, and springs
M. For silver-plated instruments:
    1. Silver polish
    2. Tarn-X
    3. Jewelers cloth
    4. Extra "clean" wiping cloth

All the above items need not be carried with the instrument at all times, but they should all be readily available.

Proper care of instruments should be taught as conscientiously as all other aspects of music instruction. The purchase and ownership of a musical instrument is a wise and valuable investment (for the serious student it is a necessity). Protect that investment and assure maximum benefits from it by maintaining its value with proper care.

Chapter 8

CAREER PREPARATION

Selecting a College, or University

Fortunately, the world abounds with great conservatories and schools of music. For the tuba player there are, worldwide, perhaps 150 fine schools where you can have applied study with a performer/teacher of high quality (ninety plus schools in the United States). Also, competition for students is such that the climate for scholarships and financial aid is very good. For the euphonium the opportunities for study with a performer/teacher on the conservatory/college level is limited. However, there are a few institutions with euphonium artist-teachers and some others with excellent tuba/euphonium or trombone/euphonium professors. Students may be encouraged to double major in euphonium and tuba or euphonium and trombone (all three are worth considering if commercial studio work is a goal). Aspiring students should obtain catalogs and application materials from those schools that interest them, and, in consultation with their high school music teacher, private teacher, and parents, select two or three schools (with favored applied teachers) for personal visits, auditions, and interviews. Remember, the better you play, the better reception you will receive. Tuba and euphonium players should realize that the extra practice time given to their instrument during high school will be monetarily compensated for in the form of college scholarship funds (for outstanding performance). In this regard, the scholarship payment for practicing will exceed that of babysitting, bagging groceries, or mowing lawns. Think about it!

Checklist

1. Applied teachers: Learn as much as you can about the person(s) from whom you will take applied lessons. Review the teacher's credentials with your high school teacher, your local private teacher, your parents. If there is a local

professional player of your instrument, seek his advice about colleges and applied teachers. Check out several selected schools.

2. Performance opportunities: Investigate the type, number, and quality of performing ensembles at each college in which you are interested. What is the ensemble/student ratio for your instrument? Is there a structured chamber music program? Study the catalogs carefully and, when you visit a school for an audition and an interview, ask lots of questions about performing ensembles. (This is very important.)

3. Degree programs: Does the college offer a wide range of degrees? Is the degree of your special interests offered? Review the course requirements of each degree.

4. Geographic location/environment: There are so many excellent schools and teachers available, you may be able to satisfy your choice of geographic location. Do you want to be in the center of a major city, or do you prefer to be in a smaller community? Do you wish to attend a school with a large music (and other) enrollment, or do you prefer a smaller school? What environment do you prefer?

5. Tuition costs/scholarships: Review with your parents the cost of tuition (in state, out of state), and the amount of scholarship and financial aid offered by each school. Be sure to check the bottom line costs with your parents. Some schools may offer a large scholarship, but net tuition costs may be double (or more) that of an equally good school. Don't let the flattery of a large scholarship distract you from the net tuition costs.

6. Final decision: Having made a choice, give your all to having a successful four years (or more) of study. Remember, you commence establishing your professional reputation the day you enter college for advanced training. Resolve to develop your performance abilities to their fullest, and explore your other talents for alternative careers.

Employment Opportunities in Music

As alluded to above, there is such a variety of opportunities in the music profession that anyone with an insatiable desire for a life in music should be able to have a successful career. Indeed, there is such variety and cross-disciplinary interaction that almost any individual, having been made aware of the possibilities, can analyze their own special combinations of strengths: instrumental performance (every discipline—orchestra, band, chamber music, jazz, etc.), conducting, composing, arranging, copying/autography/editing, teaching (public/private schools, college/university applied, composition/theory, other combinations), administration, management, public relations, marketing, sales, service, instrument repair, and so forth.

Performance

Orchestra: The potential of a performance career with a major symphony orchestra is a primary goal of virtually every young tuba player. It is a worthy goal and if it is to be realized requires concentration and rigorous preparation. Those who aspire for a symphony career cannot allow attention to be diverted from that goal. The opportunities are limited and the competition keen.

Military band: The potential of a performance career with a major service band is a primary goal of euphonium and tuba players. It is another worthy goal that requires focused concentration and rigorous preparation. As with a symphony orchestra, you must not allow your attention to be diverted from your goals. The opportunities are limited and the competition keen.

Chamber music/miscellaneous ensembles: The potential of a performance career with a major chamber ensemble or jazz ensemble is a goal of some tuba and euphonium players. Requirements for these career options are just as rigorous as those of the symphony orchestra and service band. However, contrary to the orchestra or service band, in chamber music or jazz it is possible for a performing instrumentalist who also has organizational, managerial, and marketing skills to organize, establish, and succeed with their own ensemble.

Audition preparation: The first and most important goal is to master your instrument to the best of your ability. Mastering the tuba and euphonium requires a solid foundation of basics:

1. Correct embouchure for the complete range of your instrument.

2. Full, clear, rich tone in all registers; consistent breath support is essential.

3. Complete knowledge and mastery of all scales and arpeggios, which should be memorized.

4. Constant improvement of dynamic control in all registers.

5. Solid skills in sight-reading of all types of rhythms from the traditional to jazz to contemporary idioms.

6. Complete knowledge and mastery of the basic literature for the symphony orchestra, band, chamber music (brass quintet, etc.), and/or ensembles. If jazz is your specialty, you must be fluid in jazz repertoire and styles.

7. Accurate intonation throughout your total range.

8. Endurance to meet all professional situations.

Please note: There is no personal satisfaction to compare with performing well on your chosen instrument. Needless to say, the higher artistic performance standards you achieve, the more pleasure you will derive for yourself and others. It is appropriate and essential for every applied student to aim high, to set specific and idealistic goals in performance, and to become the very best performing artist possible. It is also appropriate and important to be aware of existing conditions and to prepare for alternative income from disciplines outside the performance arena (i.e., the salary you might earn as a symphony orchestra musician or college professor can be 100 percent of your income or it can be 80 percent or another percentage of your total income. It simply depends on what else you have to offer).

Maintain your performance abilities on your instrument and gain public/professional recognition, personal satisfaction, and income. Be ever ready for opportunities that could utilize your personal interests and expertise. Learn to recognize opportunities, for they often come like a bolt of lightning and must be seized quickly before they disappear, taken by someone else. Don't be guilty of missing a great opportunity because you are unprepared, whether in performance or otherwise.

Applied Teaching Opportunities

Over years of teaching applied music students, one learns many lessons about people and life. Each separate teaching experience gives new insight to that which motivates or deters response and growth in a student. Gaining the confidence and respect of each student is a prerequisite to effective applied teaching. This one-on-one relationship requires mutual respect and understanding. Applied teaching is a partnership of two individuals pursuing the same goals, goals that serve the best interests of the student.

To achieve success with each partnership, the applied teacher must sort out, evaluate, and respond to the complexities that compose the psyche and personality of each student. The quicker this can be accomplished, the more effective the teaching will be. The base degrees of talent and potential possessed by each student can be ascertained quickly, as both are audibly and visibly demonstrated. Musical growth and improvement of instrumental techniques are likewise easily observed. Not so easily discernible is the inner turmoil of personal problems and concerns that, gone unchecked or unresolved, may prevent a student from ever realizing his talent and potential.

Resolving changes in the attitude, personality, and goals of a student, as he or she matures and is influenced or succumbs to pressures and experiences outside the studio is another responsibility of the applied teacher. Discussing and resolving ongoing concerns of each student is essential to maximum effectiveness as an applied teacher. Outside professional help may sometimes be required and should be sought when appropriate.

Talented, well-motivated students are a joy to teach. They pursue their studies steadily and with purpose; their lessons are always well-prepared. They are confident about attaining their stated goal, to succeed as professional performers. They have the talent, the heart, and the commitment. They are not dissuaded by any adversity and, to the contrary, seem to be tempered and strengthened by each experience. Obviously, not every student is so fortunate. To paraphrase a quote from the master teacher Philip Farkas: "Some students anyone can teach; they are so talented, so self-determined and so self-motivated, they absorb, assimilate and grow with every lesson, with every experience. They are the most successful of students. Some students no one can teach, they have little or no talent, and no self-esteem, they don't apply themselves, their lessons are never prepared, and no teacher, no matter how experienced he may be, will be able to reach them. Some students you must learn to teach; you must probe and determine what approaches will awaken their talents, trigger their interest, understanding and inspire self-determination. Success with these students is the most rewarding of teaching experiences."[1]

Applied teachers and students are continually reminded of the level of artistry that must be achieved and maintained for professional success as a performer through live performances and recordings. It is therefore obvious and essential that applied teachers counsel and guide their students into music careers that best suit their special abilities and interests. Any student who is truly committed to a career in music can have a successful career. However, their career may not be primarily as a performer or teacher. There are myriads of opportunities for those who aspire to a career in music. Publicly, the most visible career in music is in performance and the second most visible is in teaching. But even these two categories include many variations of opportunities. Also important to be considered are the areas of (music) arts administration, management, business, and services. Oftentimes an individual's multiple interests, talents, and skills compel a multifaceted career, a "custommade" combination career. Sometimes such multicareers evolve from a successful performance career and/or teaching career, and sometimes they are initiated with the first postgraduate position.

More and more, multiple opportunities are being created by the increasing popularity of chamber music ensembles. Faculty artists-in-residence programs for string quartets, woodwind quintets, brass quintets, percussion trios, and other ensembles offer a real bonus to many university schools of music by providing applied teachers who also perform professionally in faculty ensemble performances, both on and off campus. They represent the school at professional conferences, provide good public relations, generate public financial support, and, perhaps most importantly, recruit outstanding student instrumentalists. The applied teacher/chamber music artist is but one of the many possible combinations offered by academia. Suffice it to say, it is important that applied teachers be as versed as possible in career opportunities available in music and that they be capable of giving career guidance to applied students as they prepare to enter the profession. It is not enough to pass on performance skills and to nurture only the performance talents of students. Their ability to earn a living in music as musicians or in some combination of acquired skills is the bottom line. It behooves the students (hopefully with concerned and astute guidance of both faculty and administration) to assess their performance potential for employment, to be aware of other areas in which they are strong, and to develop their full potential for a successful career in music.

If you are well educated and knowledgeable about the art of music you will have earned credibility among your peers and colleagues and public audience. Your potential for employment in the field of music education is enhanced.

Preparation for a performance career and knowledge about how to prepare for auditions in the various performance disciplines, knowing what makes a good contract and how to negotiate, and being sensitive to the (unwritten) ethics of the profession of music will give

Summary: The Art, Profession, and Business of Music

you maximum potential for involvement and participation as a professional musician.

Learning the prerequisites and procedures of administration, management, marketing, sales, publishing, recording industry, and so forth, in combination with your knowledge of the art of music and the business of music will help you gain the best potential for security in music. To summarize: Learn the art of music for credibility, the profession of music for involvement and participation, and the business of music for security.

Footnotes

1. Philip Farkas, lecture presented at Keystone Brass Institute, Keystone, Colo., June 19, 1991.

APPENDIX A

Selected Euphonium Methods and Materials*   *Part I*

BEGINNER (GRADE SCHOOL TO JUNIOR HIGH LEVEL)

Arban, Prescott. *Arbans Famous Method Vol. I for Trombone and Baritone.* (Carl Fischer)
Most exercises based on scales and arpeggios; starts at beginning level but moves quickly. Good fundamental information based on learning basic patterns.

Arban, Prescott. *First and Second Year.* (Carl Fischer)
Excellent scales, slurs, and technique studies.

Beeler. *Method for Baritone Vol. I.* (Remick)
Some information at beginning; lists rudiments of music; helpful comments. Well-planned presentation with helpful pictures.

Beeler, *Play Away for Baritone.* (Remick)
Good, especially for the young beginner.

Cimera, Hovey. *Method for Baritone.* (Belwin)
Many helpful hints. Most exercises with stylistic markings.

Colin. *Melodious Fundamentals for Trombone (Baritone).* (Colin)
Good information on rhythm and counting with stylistic markings. Each lesson has slurs, melodies, tonguing; well-organized.

Getchell, Hovey. *First Book of Practical Studies.* (Remick)
Sixty relatively easy, short rhythmic studies in the middle range. Five pages of scale exercises in the back of the book.

Herfurth, Miller. *A Tune a Day for Baritone.* (Belwin)
Excellent for beginner. Moves slowly with good pictures.

Hovey. *Elementary Method.* (Rubank)
Methodical method that moves slowly.

Kinyon. *Breeze Easy for Baritone.* (Witmark)
Book moves very slowly with many songs.

Prescott. *Prep Band Method.* (Schmitt, Hall & McCreary)
Excellent beginners book. It employs good pedagogy. Uses fine melodies from well-known symphonic literature.

Sueta. *Band Method Book I.* (Macie Publishing Company)
Features famous melodies from operas and symphonies. Includes easy duets.

INTERMEDIATE (JUNIOR HIGH TO HIGH SCHOOL)

Arban, Bell. *Interpretations of Arbans Method.* (Colin)
Excellent method for proper articulations and finger slurs for the euphonium. Based on scales and arpeggios with double and triple tongue exercises.

Arban, Randall, and Mantia. *Arbans Famous Method Vol. I & II.* (Carl Fischer)
Most exercises based on scales and arpeggios. Good fundamental information based on learning basic patterns.

Arban, Whistler. *Modern Arban Comprehensive Course for Trombone and Baritone.* (Rubank)
Good arrangement of materials; moves fast and would have to be supplemented for most students. Some literature with a few double and triple tongue exercises.

Beeler. *Method for Baritone Vol. II.* (Remick)
Fine method with double and triple tongue work. Good comments and helpful hints.

Clarke. *Technical Studies.* (Carl Fischer)
Good solid technique studies based on the famous cornet studies of Herbert Clarke.

Enderssen. *Supplementary Studies.* (Rubank)
Studies in the middle range of the baritone/euphonium.

Fink. *From Treble to Bass Clef Baritone.* (Accura Music)
Excellent study to help student transfer from treble to bass clef.

Getchell. *Second Book of Practical Studies.* (Belwin)
Fifty-three rhythmic studies in the middle range of the baritone/euphonium.

Sueta. *Band Method Book II & III.* (Macie Publishing Company)
Features melodies from famous symphonies and operas. Stays in the middle range using various keys and duets.

Vandercook. Studies for the Trombone and Baritone. (Rubank)
Good exercises for the young baritone player from easy-medium to medium level.

Voxman and Gower. *Advanced Method for Baritone Vol. I & II.* (Rubank)
Good exercises with scales, arpeggios, phrasing, embellishments, and group tonguing.

Whistler. *Modern Pares.* (Rubank)
Excellent for developing articulation throughout the various scale patterns. Habituates scale fingering in a hurry.

ADVANCED (HIGH SCHOOL TO COLLEGE TO PROFESSIONAL)

Arban, Randall, and Mantia. *Arbans Famous Method Vol. I & II.* (Carl Fischer)
Basically all technique with some helpful information of melodic embellishments, double and triple tongue work, and several theme and variations and cadenzas.

Bernard. *Methode Complete Pour Trombone, Basse.* (Leduc)
Very thorough method; covers everything. Mainly for French tuba; usable for baritone/euphonium.

Bordogni, Rochut. *Melodious Etudes Vol. I, II, & III.* (Carl Fischer)
Edited for trombone. Fine legato studies; phrasing well-marked; romantic era music; good study for endurance, especially in Vol. II & III because of the high tessitura.

Brasch. *The Euphonium and Four-Valve Brasses.* (Harold Brasch Publications)
Excellent introduction to the use of the fourth valve.

Goethe, Ostrander. *60 Studies.* (International)
Highly chromatic book that uses very difficult rhythms. A good help to approach contemporary music.

Kropprasch, Fote. *60 Selected Studies Vol. I & II.* (Carl Fischer)
Sixty etudes covering a relatively wide range as well as a variety of key signatures. Generally good for phrasing study. A standard for horns, baritones/euphoniums, trombones, and tubas.

Ostrander. *The F Attachment and Bass Trombone.* (Colin)
Good book for four-valve euphonium. Moves quickly but is thorough, most exercises short.

Slema. *66 Studies in All Keys for Trombone.* (International)
Excellent book for good euphonium player. Often no place to breathe; lots of work in middle and low range with variations in style. Highly chromatic studies that prepare the player for contemporary sound.

Tyrell. *40 Progressive Studies.* (Boosey & Hawkes)
Forty etudes for the intermediate to advanced student with primarily flat keys, with some rhythmic variety utilizing basically the middle register of the euphonium. This method is designed for band musicians. Good exercises for the tongue.

Voxman. *Selected Studies.* (Rubank)
Twenty-six etudes for studies in both tonguing and legato style. Quality of music good throughout; includes velocity studies and cadenza studies.

Selected Tuba Methods and Materials*

Part II

BEGINNER (GRADE SCHOOL TO JUNIOR HIGH LEVEL)
Arban, Prescott. *First and Second Year.* (Fischer)
Excellent scales, slurs, and technique studies.

Beeler. *Method for Tuba.* (Remick)
Contains valuable pictures. Strong on lip slurs, warm-up, and rhythmical treatment. Familiar melodies and duets. Contains a good beginning in sharp keys.

Beeler. *Play Away for Tuba or Sousaphone.* (Schirmer)
Good, especially for the young beginner. Contains a little theory.

Getchell. *First Book for Practical Studies.* (Belwin)
Sixty relatively easy, short rhythmic studies in flat keys only in the middle range of the BB-flat tuba. Five pages of scale exercises in the back of the book.

Herfurth, Miller. *A Tune a Day for Tuba.* (Boston Music)
Excellent for a beginner. Moves slowly. Contains good pictures.

Hovey. *Elementary Method.* (Rubank)
The method covers the material needed by an elementary student in slow methodical sequence.

Pease. *Bass Method, Book I.* (Pro Art)
Strong beginning method. Good pictures. Parts of the instrument are labeled.

Prescott. *Prep Band Method.* (Schmitt, Hall & McCreary)
Excellent beginners book. It employs pedagogy by utilizing any new notes and theory that are learned. Melodies from well-known symphonic literature.

Sueta. *Band Method Book I.* (Macie Publishing Company)
Features famous melodies from operas and symphonies. Includes easy duets.

INTERMEDIATE (JUNIOR HIGH TO HIGH SCHOOL)

Arban, Bell. *Interpretations of Arban Method.* (Colin)
Excellent introduction to the famous Arban brass method. Covers articulations and fingered slurs adapted to the tuba. For the serious high school student.

Beeler. *Method for BB-flat Tuba Book II.* (Remick)
Good for high school students. Emphasis on low register and lip slurs. Selections from opera, symphonic poems, and so forth.

Bell. *Foundation to Tuba and Sousaphone Playing.* (Carl Fischer)
Excellent treatment of articulation and lip slurs. Meant for the serious high school player. Includes band excerpts tuba solos.

Blazhevich. *70 Studies for BB-flat Tuba Vol. I.* (Robert King)
For the serious high school student. These studies are melodious and contain good examples of mixed meter, intricate rhythms, and phrasing.

Brightmore. *Studies for Brass.* (Chappell)
Bass clef edition. Intermediate material that pushes the range. Short studies require solid sound and support and careful phrasing for success.

Cimera. *73 Advanced Tuba Studies.* (Belwin)
For the serious high school student. Etudes in a variety of rhythms and keys. Covers relatively wide range for BB-flat and CC tubas.

Eby. *Scientific Methods I & II.* (Jacobs)
Good overall method for the serious developing tuba player.

Endressen. *Supplementary Studies.* (Rubank)
Forty-five studies, mostly in flats in the middle range of the BB-flat (CC) tuba. Includes a chart for E-flat and BB-flat tuba.

Fink. *Studies in Legato.* (Carl Fischer)
Originally conceived for the trombone vocalise of Concone, Marchesi, and Fanofka. Excellent legato study for the tuba, but all in the easy range. Well-edited in regard to breathing and phrasing.

Geib. *Geib Method for Tuba.* (Carl Fischer)
Designed to be a complete method from beginning to advanced with three sections: long tones, tonguing, and orchestral studies. Meant for the more serious or high school student.

Getchell. *Second Book of Practical Studies.* (Belwin)
Fifty-three rhythmic studies (mostly flat keys) in the middle range of the tuba. Etudes are slightly longer and somewhat more advanced than book one.

Hedja. *Etudes.* (Boosey & Hawkes)
Twenty-two studies in primarily flat keys covering the middle range of the tuba.

Jacobs. Special section in back of *Hal Leonard Advanced Band Method.* (Hal Leonard)
Arnold Jacobs wrote this "all in a nutshell" section for the intermediate to advanced student.

Kopprasch. *60 Selected Studies.* (Robert King)
For the serious high school student. Sixty etudes covering a relatively wide range for the tuba as well as a variety of key signatures. Generally good for phrasing study.

Kuehn. *60 Selected Studies Book I & II.* (Robert King)
From vocalises of Concone and Marchesi. Excellent legato material for the intermediate to advanced students with long phrases for the lower range of the tuba. Does for the tuba player what Rochut does for the trombonist. Includes five flats and five sharps.

Slema. *66 Etudes.* (Carl Fischer)
An intermediate student could begin with this book, but it gets quite difficult. This book, for bass clef instruments and written in trombone range, begins with no flats or sharps and adds one flat or sharp at a time to seven sharps or flats. The student will have to play an octave lower than written.

Sueta. *Band Method Books II–III.* (Macie Publishing Company)
Includes melodies from famous symphonies and operas as well as duets. Stays in easy middle range while encouraging the player to perform in different keys and various rhythmic patterns.

Tyrell. *Advanced Studies.* (Boosey & Hawkes)
Forty etudes for the intermediate to advanced student with primarily flat keys with some rhythmic variety utilizing basically the middle register of the tuba. This method is designed for band musicians. Good exercises for the tongue.

Vandercook. *Studies for E♭ or BB♭ Bass.* (Rubank)
For the young tuba player from easy-medium to medium-intermediate level.

Voxman and Gower. *Advanced Method for E♭ and BB♭ Bass.* (Rubank)

Covers scales and arpeggios, phrasing, embellishments, group tonguing. Intermediate level, although labeled advanced. The book represents a complete method of development.

Whistler. *Modern Pares.* (Rubank)
Excellent for developing rapid articulation throughout the various scale patterns. Habituates scale fingering in a hurry.

ADVANCED (HIGH SCHOOL TO COLLEGE TO PROFESSIONAL)

Arban, Bell. *Complete Method.* (Colin)
Includes warm-ups and daily routine, Blazhevich interpretations, Arban interpretations, and artistic solos and duets.

Bell. *Tuba Warm-Ups.* (Colin)
Long tone exercise is excellent. Includes double and triple tonguing. Scale and arpeggio studies are for the advanced student. Extended routine for the serious tuba player.

Bernard. *40 Etudos pour Tuba.* (Leduc)
A good variety of keys, rhythms, and articulations. Written for BB-flat and CC tubas. Contains mordents, trills, turns, and embellishments.

Blazhevich. *70 Studies for BBb Tuba Vol. I & II.* (Robert King)
Plenty of variety in keys that are mostly technical and work on extension of range. Extremely valuable for the serious tuba player. Exercise 70 is a great one for those who wish to practice sniff breathing.

Cimera. *73 Advanced Tuba Studies.* (Belwin)
Seventy-three etudes in a variety of rhythms and keys. Covers relatively wide range for BB-flat and CC tubas.

Delgiudice. *Dix Petits Textes.* (Eschig)
Ten little solos or supplementary study material for the extreme ranges. Has piano accompaniment. Undoubtedly for the F tuba, but a real challenge for the advanced player on the larger tubas.

Fink. *Studies in Legato.* (Carl Fischer)
Based on the vocalise of Concone, Marchesi, and Fanofka. Excellent legato study for the tuba, all in the easy range.

Fitch. *Rhythmical Articulation.* (Carl Fischer)
Parts II and III from the Complete Method by Pasquale Bona. Can be played as written or an octave lower. Challenge in developing the upper register—good for F or E-flat tuba.

Gallay. *30 Studies.* (Robert King)
Original horn studies for developing musicianship. Consideration for phrasing and style is in each study.

Knaub. *Progressive Techniques for Tuba.* (Belwin)
Roughly 80 percent of book includes the seventy etudes for tuba of Blazhevich. Includes a daily routine for the tuba player plus the harmonic series for F, E-flat, BB-flat, CC tubas, fourth and fifth valve harmonic series, and a chart of fingerings for E-flat and BB-flat compensating instruments.

Kopprasch. *60 Selected Studies.* (Robert King)
A standard for horns, trombones, and tubas. Sixty etudes covering a relatively wide range for tuba as well as a variety of key signatures.

Kuehn. *28 Advanced Studies.* (Southern Music Company)
From the vocalise of Ferdinand Sieber. An excellent follow-up to *Sixty Musical Studies for Tuba* by David Kuehn

Lachman. *25 Etudes.* (Hofmeister)
Excellent for developing and controlling upper register. Undoubtedly written for an F tuba, but good study for the lower keyed tubas.

Lachman. *26 Etudes.* (Hofmeister)
Very musical studies worthy of an accompaniment. A study for every major and minor key.

Laenz. *Zwolf Spezialstudien for Tuba.* (Hofmeister)
An excellent book to follow the Blazhevich studies. One of the best for reading contemporary intervals. High range.

Roberts. *43 Bel Canto Studies for Tuba.* (Robert King)
This is based on the Marco Bordogni vocalise. Introductory remarks and footnotes are great for sound musicianship.

Sear. *Etudes for Tuba.* (Cor)
Forty-three melodic etudes in a variety of keys and time signatures covering a wide range for the tuba. At the end are several excerpts from the Bach Cello Suites.

Slema. *66 Etudes.* (Carl Fischer)
Written in the trombone range with etudes that are quite melodious. Could be played an octave lower.

Uber. *Concert Etudes.* (Southern)
Good variety of stylistic considerations with excellent rhythmic etudes.

Vasiliev. *24 Melodious Etudes for Tuba.* (Robert King)
Studies in a variety of keys covering a relatively wide range. Emphasis on difficult intervals in many of the etudes. Contains a variety of styles.

*There are several other good methods and study books for the euphonium and tuba. Many players use various materials from other instruments such as the horn, trumpet (treble clef), and trombone (bass clef, tenor clef, and alto clef). Most of the books, methods, and study books suggested for euphonium are written in bass clef.

Instrument Manufacturers and Distributors in the United States

Part III

Alexander Brothers (Germany), distributed by Custom Music Company, 1414 South Main Street, Royal Oak, Michigan 48067

Amati (Czechoslovakia), distributed by Giardenelli, 151 West 46th Street, New York, New York 10036

Besson (England), distributed by Boosey & Hawkes, Inc., P.O. Box 130, Oceanside, New York 11572

Boehm & Meinl (Germany), distributed by Deg Music Products, P.O. Box 408, Lake Geneva, Wisconsin 43147

B & S (Germany), distributed by Custom Music Company, 1414 South Main Street, Royal Oak, Michigan 48067

B & S (Germany), distributed by Giardenelli, 151 West 46th Street, New York, New York 10036

C. G. Conn Ltd., 1000 Industrial Parkway, Elkhart, Indiana 45516

Courtois (France), distributed by Leblanc, 7019 Thirtieth Ave., Kenosha, Wisconsin 53141

Deg Music Product, P.O. Box 408, Lake Geneva, Wisconsin 43147

Getzen, P.O. Box 459, Elkhorn, Wisconsin 53121-0459

Hirsbrunner (Switzerland), distributed by Custom Music Company, 1414 South Main Street, Royal Oak, Michigan 48067

Holton, distributed by Leblanc, 7019 Thirtieth Ave., Kenosha, Wisconsin 53141

Kalison (Italian), distributed by The Tuba Exchange, 1825 Chapel Hill Road, Durham, North Carolina 27707

King Musical Instruments, Curtis Blvd., Eastlake, Ohio 44094

Jupiter (Taiwan), distributed by Jupiter Band Instruments, P.O. Box 90249, Austin, Texas 78709-0249

Meinl-Weston (Germany), distributed by Getzen, P.O. Box 459, Elkhorn, Wisconsin 53121-0459

Mirafone (Germany), distributed by Mirafone, P.O. Box 909, Sun Valley, California 91352

Peratucci/B & S (Germany), distributed by Custom Music Company, 1414 South Main Street, Royal Oak, Michigan 48067

Rudolf Meinl (Germany), distributed by Custom Music Company, 1414 South Main Street, Royal Oak, Michigan 48067

Sanders/V. C. Cerveny (Czechoslovakia), distributed by Custom Music Company, 1414 South Main Street, Royal Oak, Michigan 48067

Sear/Cerveny (Czechoslovakia), distributed by Sear Sound, 235 West 46th Street, New York, New York 10036

Sear/Deprins (Belgium), distributed by Sear Sound, 235 West 46th Street, New York, New York 10036

Selmar, P.O. Box 310, Elkhart, Indiana 46515

United Musical Instruments (Parent Company of C. G. Conn and King Musical Instruments), 1000 Industrial Parkway, Elkhart, Indiana 46516

Willson (Switzerland), distributed by Deg Music Products, Box 468, Lake Geneva, Wisconsin 43147

Yamaha (Japan), distributed by Yamaha Musical Instrument Corporation, 3445 East Paris Avenue, S.E. P.O. Box 899, Grand Rapids, MI 49512-0899, USA

Special Acknowledgments/Consultants

Edwin "Buddy" Baker
William Bell
Arthur Benade
Roger Bobo
Brian Bowman
Harold Brasch
Barton Cummings
Shelley Dragoo
Brent Dutton
Mike Eastep
Phillip Farkas
Jack Herrick
Rodney Hudson
Arnold Jacobs
Edward Kleinhammer

David Kuehn
Andre Larson
Arne B. Larson
Earle Louder
R. Winston Morris
Robert J. Pallansch
Daniel Perantoni
Jack Robinson
Lewis Roth
Gunther Schuller
Walter Sears
Robert Tucci
Les Varner
Kenneth Winkle
Curtis Wood

Great Artists of the Euphonium and Tuba Heritage (Representative List)

Ashley Alexander—Euphonium (1936–1988)
Russell Alexander—Euphonium (1877–1915)
William J. Bell—Tuba (1902–1971)
Harold Brasch—Euphonium (1916–1984)
George Black—Tuba (1897–1988)
Philip Cadway—Tuba
Philip Catelinet—Tuba (1910–   )
Phillip Donatelli—Tuba
Rueben Clinton "Johnny" Evans—Tuba (1905–   )
Leonard Falcone—Euphonium (1889–1985)
John Fletcher—Tuba (1941–1987)
Salvatore Florio—Euphonium
Fritz Geib—Tuba
August Helleberg—Tuba
Noble Howard—Euphonium
John (The Chief) Kuhn—Tuba
Tony LaZizza—Tuba
Simone Mantia—Euphonium (1873–1951)
Luke Del Negro—Tuba
Fred Pfaff—Tuba
Jack Richardson—Tuba
Gabe Russ—Tuba
Jess Russ—Tuba
Kurahel Sato—Euphonium (1900–1986)
Kilton Vinal Smith—Tuba (1909–1987)
Joseph (Tarto) Tortariello—Tuba (1902–1986)
Angelo Zavarino—Tuba (1915–   )
Louis Zavarino—Tuba (1920–   )

Part IV

Part V

APPENDIX B

Part I *Pictorial Survey of the History of Instruments Before the Euphonium and Tuba*
Pictures courtesy of
The Shrine to Music Museum
Dr. Andre Larson, Director
University of South Dakota
Vermillion, South Dakota

Part II *Pictorial Survey of the Early Euphoniums and Tubas*
Pictures courtesy of
The Shrine to Music Museum
Dr. Andre Larson, Director
University of South Dakota
Vermillion, South Dakota

Appendix B

Part I

PICTORIAL SURVEY OF THE EARLY BASS WIND INSTRUMENTS

Pictures courtesy of The Shrine to Music Museum
Dr. Andre Larson, Director
University of South Dakota
Vermillion, South Dakota

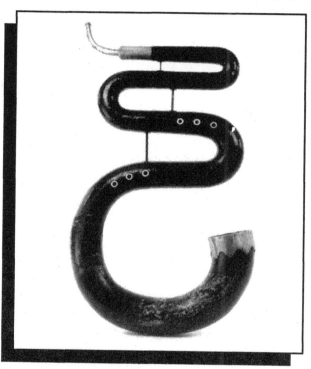

No. 1279. Serpent, England, ca. 1780-1800. Arne B. Larson Collection, 1979.

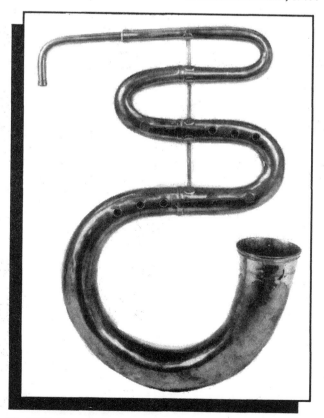

No. 2677. Serpent, England, ca. 1825-30 Copper. Rawlins Fund, 1980.

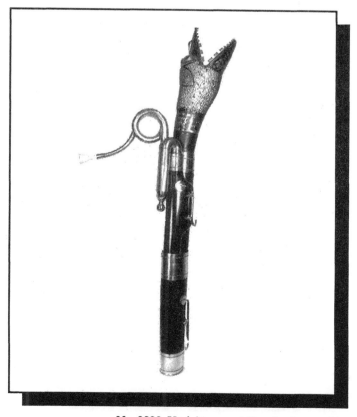

No. 2889. Upright serpent (Russian bassoon) by Sautermeister & Müller, Lyons, France, ca. 1830-40. Gift of Frederic H. & Elisabeth A. Burt & children, Jackson, Michigan, 1981.

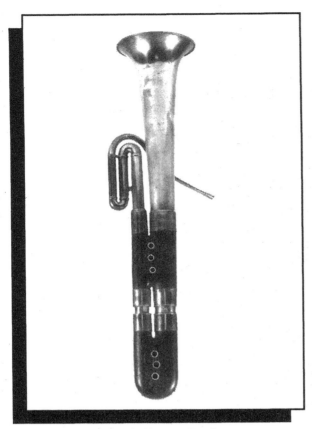

No. 2888. Ophimonocleide by Jean-Baptiste
Coeffet, Chaumont-en-Vexin, Oise, France. ca.
1828-30. Board of Trustees, 1981.

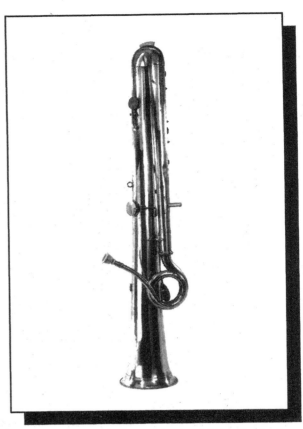

No. 2419. Ophicleide in C by Charles Pace.
London, ca. 1834-49. Ringley Fund, 1978.

No. 3127. Soprano ophicleide in B-flat by
Adolphe Sax, Paris, ca. 1850. Board of Trustees,
1982.

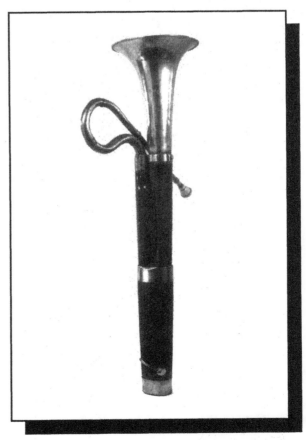

No. 1275. Upright serpent (Russian bassoon) by
P. Piana, Milan, ca. 1800. Arne B. Larson
Collection, 1979.

Appendix B

Part II

PICTORIAL SURVEY OF THE EARLY EUPHONIUMS AND TUBAS

Pictures courtesy of The Shrine to Music Museum

Dr. Andre Larson, Director
University of South Dakota
Vermillion, South Dakota

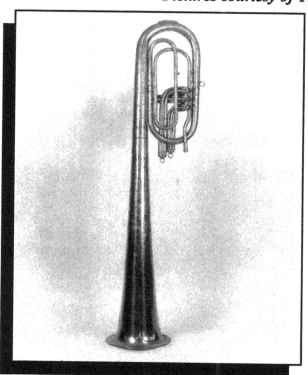

No. 316. Tuba in E-flat by John F. Stratton. New York, after 1860. Over-the-shoulder model. Arne B. Larson Collection, 1979.

No. 2362. Baritone by Henry G. Lehnert, Philadelphia, Pennsylvania, ca. 1875. Centennial model. Arne B. Larson Collection, 1979.

No. 2902. Bass tuba in F, unsigned. Germany, ca. 1848. Board of Trustees, 1981.

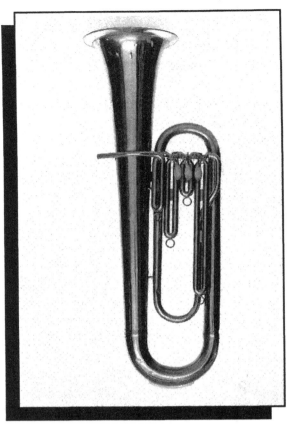

No. 247. Tuba in E-flat by Hall & Quinby,
Boston, Massachusetts, ca. 1866. Arne B. Larson
Collection, 1979.

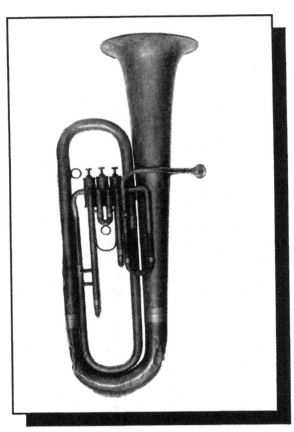

No. 311. Tuba in E-flat by Lyon & Healy,
Chicago, ca. 1869-99. Arne B. Larson Collection
1979.

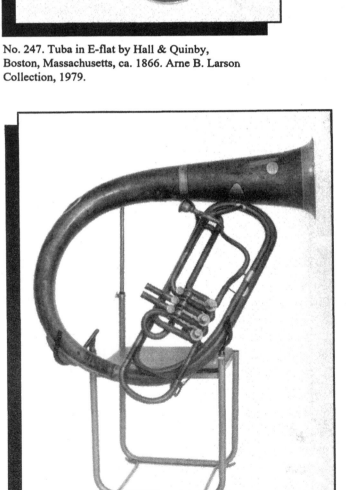

No. 313. Helicon in E-flat by Girardi Strumenti
Musicale, Naples, Italy, ca. 1880-99. Arne B.
Larson Collection, 1979.

No. 680. Helicon in E-flat by C.G. Conn
Elkhart, Indiana and Worcester, Massachusetts,
ca. 1890. Arne B. Larson Collection, 1979.

No. 643. Tuba in E-flat by A. Lecomte & Cie, Paris, ca. 1867-78. Arne B. Larson Collection, 1979.

No. 158. Helicon in BB-flat by J.W. York and Sons, Grand Rapids, Michigan, ca. 1913-17. Arne B. Larson Collection, 1979.

No. 113. Helicon in E-flat by Buescher, Elkhart, Indiana, ca. 1915. Arne B. Larson Collection, 1979.

No. 117. Tuba in E-flat by Tourville & Cie,
Paris, ca. 1880. Arne B. Larson Collection, 1979.

No. 276. Tuba in E-flat by C.G. Conn, Elkhart,
Indiana, and Worcester, Massachusetts, ca. 1887.
Arne B. Larson Collection, 1979.

No. 115. Tuba in E-flat by Martin Band
Instrument Company, Elkhart, Indiana, after
1910. Arne B. Larson Collection, 1979.

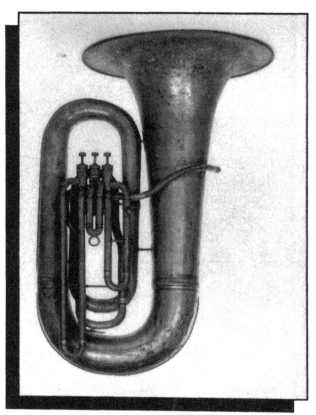

No. 138. Tuba in E-flat by J.W. York & Sons,
Grand Rapids, Michigan, ca. 1917-21. Arne B.
Larson Collection, 1979.

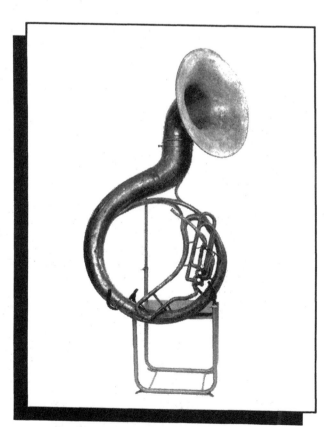

No. 1225. Sousaphone in E-flat by Keffer,
Williamsport, Pennsylvania, ca. 1939. Arne B.
Larson Collection, 1979.

No. 2204. Double-bell euphonium by C.G.
Conn, Elkhart, Indiana, ca. 1903 Arne B. Larson
Collection, 1979.

No. 363. Tuba in BB-flat (recording bass) by C.
G. Conn, Ltd., Elkhart, Indiana, ca. 1934. Model
22J. Arne B. Larson Collection, 1979.

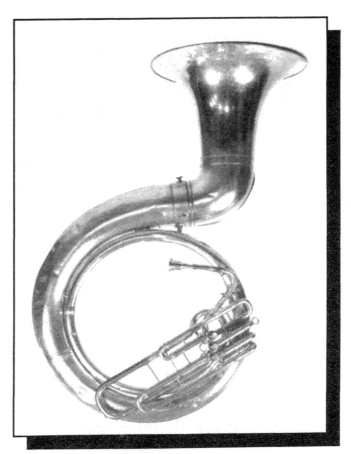

No. 335. Sousaphone in BB-flat by C.G. Conn,
Elkhart, Indiana, ca. 1904. Raincatcher model.
Arne B. Larson Collection, 1979.